AL
DUI

MONEY GUIDES

LEAVING YOUR
MONEY WISELY

ALLIED
DUNBAR

MONEY GUIDES

LEAVING YOUR MONEY WISELY

Tony Foreman

Longman

© Allied Dunbar Financial Services Limited 1988

ISBN 0–85121–381–2

Published by

Longman Professional and Business Communication Division
Longman Group UK Limited
21–27 Lamb's Conduit Street, London WC1N 3NJ

Associated Offices

Australia	Longman Professional Publishing (Pty) Limited 130 Phillip Street, Sydney, NSW 2000
Hong Kong	Longman Group (Far East) Limited Cornwall House, 18th Floor, Taikoo Trading Estate, Tong Chong Street, Quarry Bay
Malaysia	Longman Malaysia Sdn Bhd No 3 Jalan Kilang A, Off Jalan Penchala, Petaling Jaya, Selangor, Malaysia
Singapore	Longman Singapore Publishers (Pte) Ltd 25 First Lok Yang Road, Singapore 2262
USA	Longman Group (USA) Inc 500 North Dearborn Street, Chicago, Illinois 60610

No responsibility for loss occasioned to any person acting or refraining from action as a result of the material in this publication can be accepted by the author or publishers.

The views and opinions of Allied Dunbar may not necessarily coincide with some of the views and opinions expressed in this book which are solely those of the author and no endorsement of them by Allied Dunbar should be inferred.

A CIP Catalogue record for this book is available from the British Library.

Printed in Great Britain by Biddles Ltd, Guildford, Surrey.

Tony Foreman

Tony Foreman has specialised in tax and personal financial planning for 20 years. His career has included periods with the Inland Revenue, two leading firms of chartered accountants, a merchant bank and a large firm of stockbrokers

He is currently the Director of Personal Financial Planning Services in Pannell Kerr Forster's London Office.

Contents

9 What can be done? The scope for taking action

1 Introduction

There's nothing so certain in the world as death and taxes.
Benjamin Franklin

This book is all about leaving your money wisely. Having worked for it, you now want to make sure that it passes on to your family and your heirs when you are no longer around to look after them yourself.

However, there is just one thing which stands in your way – and that is inheritance tax. This is a relatively new tax introduced in the Finance Act of 1986. It replaced capital transfer tax which itself had replaced estate duty in 1975.

The concept of taxation has been with us for years. Nearly 2,000 years ago, Caesar Augustus sent out a decree 'that all the world should be taxed', an admirable precedent which is dear to the heart of every British Chancellor. Taxation was initially introduced as a means of raising money to cover Government expenditure but it is now used increasingly to bring about social change with 'redistribution of wealth' being a popular cry.

One of the most potent ways of redistributing wealth is by way of capital taxation – that is, a taxation on capital. This is what inheritance tax is. Capital taxation is here to stay because although the various political parties may disagree on the extent to which capital should be taxed, they are all in broad agreement that it must be taxed.

Inheritance tax is, of course, essentially a tax that arises on death, which makes Benjamin Franklin's observation doubly apposite. Many people think that death duties are a modern tax but they are not – estate duty dates back to 1881.

The overall objective of death duties is to prevent the passing on of large estates by inheritance. As a consequence, inheritance tax tends to come into its own on death although, like all other taxes, there is no need for anybody to pay more than necessary. Within limits, everyone is entitled to organise his or her affairs in such a way that their tax liability is reduced – there is no obligation on anybody to pay more than their fair share.

The present form of inheritance tax can be summed up in a few simple statements. It's important to stress at this stage that these *are* simple statements and they are there as a guide, not as a definitive statement of the way inheritance tax works.

1   Inheritance tax bites when you dispose of your property other than to your spouse. It is principally designed to tax property passing on to your heirs when you die.
2   One way around inheritance tax might appear to be to give it away before you die. You can do that – but only up to a point. Gifts are taxed as well. There is a range of gifts you can make which will allow you to reduce your estate but only over a period of time.
3   If you give property away, you lose control. Trusts can be a simple way of giving it away and retaining control at the same time. However, you can't give it away and retain the benefit – that's not allowed.
4   The family home can often be your largest asset. There are some simple precautions you can take to make sure it doesn't have to be sold to pay a tax bill.
5   Businesses are often 'given away' on death – which could be very unfair if they were taxed heavily as a result. A lifetime's work could be handed to the taxman which isn't the point of inheritance tax. There are therefore some special reliefs for businesses.
6   There are some simple plans you can make in advance. A correctly drafted Will can save some tax and a simple life

assurance policy could provide the funds to pay the remainder.

One of the dangers with inheritance tax lies in its very name. The majority of people probably don't regard themselves as wealthy and tend to ignore the things which are associated with 'inheritances' and 'estates'. However, that is false thinking. As we will see, even fairly modest estates can attract the attention of the taxman because inheritance tax starts to bite at a relatively low level. There are, for example, many people living in London or its surroundings who have very modest incomes but who own a house worth £120,000, £150,000 or even £200,000. Inheritance tax starts at £110,000 so although these people may only pay basic rate income tax, on their deaths, the State will charge 40% inheritance tax on the top slice of their estates – the same rate that is paid by a millionaire.

The rates of tax have, however, recently been reduced. In 1974 Mr Healey introduced capital transfer tax by saying that 'it would squeeze the rich until the pips squeak'. The tax started at 30% for estates in excess of £15,000 and rose fairly rapidly to a top rate of 75%. At present, such tax is charged at a flat rate of 40%.

Nevertheless, although rates of tax have been reduced, that has to be seen in the context of comparing present rates with those in force over the last 20 years. After all, your grandparents (who might have grown up in Victorian or Edwardian Britain) would have thought it absolutely outrageous for the State to take up to 40% of a family's wealth on death. Furthermore, they would have regarded estate duty as something which concerned only the extremely rich whereas inheritance tax now affects people who probably wouldn't even regard themselves as moderately well off.

The book is, in effect, in four parts:

1   In the first part, we look at how a liability to inheritance tax can arise at all. We will cover the ways in which it

can be reduced (there's a chapter devoted to how you can give your property away without incurring a tax bill) but the main topics will be to show you how a liability can arise.

2   In the second section, we look at what you can do to reduce the problem. Most of this will assume that you still have to live, ie you can't give it all away. So, just what can you do to ensure your independence and at the same time ensure a low tax bill for your heirs?

3   In the third section we look at some special cases. Single or divorced people have their own particular problems and we also look at the needs of non-British people and expatriots.

4   In the final section we cover the way the tax is actually paid and how the Revenue keep us all under control.

Finally, at the end of the book, there's a glossary of some of the terms used.

A word about trusts

Throughout this book we will refer from time to time to the use of trusts. There are few words in financial planning circles that are more misunderstood and feared. Most people have no idea what a trust is but associate it in some way with substantial wealth and with, perhaps, a whiff of tax-evasion.

Nothing could be further from the truth. Trusts can be a very straightforward way of arranging your affairs so that things happen that *you* want to happen. In many ways, therefore, they are like Wills.

Consider for a moment what a Will is. It is a straightforward statement of your wishes regarding what happens to your property when you die. If you want your nephew to receive £1,000 then you put that in your Will and it will happen. A

Will is a binding legal document with the full weight of the law behind you.

Many people get nervous about making a Will simply because of this legal aspect – it makes it all seem a little daunting. In actual fact, there's no need whatsoever to use a solicitor in writing up your Will – writing your wishes on a simple piece of paper will (provided they're witnessed) be all that is needed. However, it is a very good idea to use a solicitor because their job is to ensure that your wishes are precisely expressed. In this way, there can be no doubt at all as to what you mean.

For example, if you write, 'I leave all my property in equal shares to my wife and two children,' what does this actually mean? Does it mean a third each? Or does it mean 50% to your wife and 50% to your children? A correctly drafted Will would make it clear.

A trust is similar to a Will in that it allows you to dispose of your property in the way you wish. Like a Will, there are some legal details to attend to so that there is no doubt at all as to your intentions.

What is a trust?

If you give your nephew £1,000 in cash for him to spend, it is an outright gift. You have immediately handed over £1,000 and you have no further say in what happens to it. In legal terms, you (the donor) have made a gift to your nephew (the beneficiary) *absolutely*.

But, in some cases, it may be unwise to make such a gift at the present time (your nephew may be young and unused to handling money). The gift may have no legal sense (there's little point in handing over your stocks and shares to a six-year old) or, it may be impossible (you, yourself, may not yet be the owner of the property you wish to donate).

This is where the use of trusts has evolved. They allow you to make a gift *now* in such a way that the full benefit may not take effect until some time in the future. Instead of making an outright gift to the beneficiary, you give it instead to a person or group of people who will look after the property on behalf of the beneficiaries. The trustees have to follow your instructions regarding the eventual handing over of the property and these should be legally drafted so that there are no doubts at all as to what you want to happen.

The people you ask to look after the property are called the **trustees** and the instructions they have to follow comprise the **trust deed**.

And that's all there is to it.

How does a trust work?

We can show you this with a simple example.

EXAMPLE

David and Vivien have been married for some years and they have two teenage children. David has dabbled with some success on the Stock Exchange and has built up a portfolio of shares and unit trusts. He keeps a close eye on these and manages his portfolio as best he can. It's all a bit of a mystery to Vivien (who doesn't understand stocks and shares) but the income from them is a useful addition to the household budget.

David wants to ensure that his children eventually benefit from his Stock Market success. However, he has to think of what would happen if he died first:

- If Vivien inherited them, would she know what to do with them? What if she remarried?
- If the children inherited them, will *they* know what to do with them? Will Vivien miss the income?

What David needs is a solution which will guarantee that the children *eventually* receive the shares, that the portfolio will be looked after if he's not there and that Vivien gets the income for as long as she's alive. So, he sets up a trust.

He does this by handing over his portfolio to a person or group of people he can trust (the trustees) to look after the portfolio (and there's no reason why he can't appoint *himself* as a trustee for as long as he is alive). The trustees have to act at all times in the interests of the **beneficiaries** (the people who will benefit from the trust) and David will make quite sure that the trust deed spells out what they can and cannot do —and he will use a solicitor to get the words right)

The basis of the trust is that Vivien receives the income for as long as she is alive. On her death, the portfolio passes to the children and the trust will be 'wound up'.

For David, the problem has been solved.

Types of trust

One of the problems with anything even remotely legal is that there's a whole world of jargon surrounding it. The type of trust that David has set up is called **'interest in possession'**. David is the donor. Vivien (because she in effect 'inhabits' the trust while she is alive and receives 'rent') is called the **life tenant**. His children (who get nothing until Vivien dies) have what is called a **'reversionary interest'**.

A key point about trusts is in the *difference* between a Will and a trust. They are both concerned with giving away property but Wills only take effect on death. You can change your Will as often as you want while you are alive.

Trusts, on the other hand, take effect as soon as they are set up and can be very difficult to change. If you are thinking of setting up a trust you should, therefore, be quite sure that you know what you are doing.

It would, of course, have been possible for David to set up his trust in his Will – and this would have been called a **'Will trust'**. In this way, he gets the best of both worlds — he can look after his property whilst he is alive but make the necessary arrangements to make sure that Vivien gets the income while she is alive and that his children don't lose their inheritance.

The other types of trust that we will meet throughout the book are called '**accumulation and maintenance trust**' and '**discretionary trust**'.

So, what's the point?

From the point of view of inheritance tax, there are two main considerations that will be covered in this book:

1 If you are the beneficiary under the terms of a trust set up by someone else, you own property. The value of this property could be part of your estate if you died. It's therefore important to know how the value of the trust would be calculated in order for you to estimate your potential inheritance tax bill.
2 Setting up a trust can have important consequences in reducing the inheritance tax bill on your own estate.

Consequently, on the one hand, inheritance tax has to be borne in mind if you are a beneficiary and, on the other hand, it *could* lead to you becoming a donor and setting up a trust in order to minimise the inheritance tax bill on your own estate.

Personal considerations

Inheritance tax is only one factor in sensible financial planning. There are personal considerations such as the need to secure your own and your spouse's income requirements, the desire that you have to keep your options open against the unexpected and so on. Naturally, you will wish to keep control of capital in case you need to draw on it because of inflation or, if you're elderly, to meet possible nursing home fees. This book is about leaving your money wisely, it is *not* an attempt to persuade you to take extreme steps just to avoid inheritance tax.

At the end of the day, you may choose not to take any action beyond changing your Will. That will be your choice, we certainly can't prescribe to you. Only you can weigh up the multitude of different considerations. However, many people do feel able to strike a balance and take some steps to mitigate the burden of tax without jeopardising their personal security and independence.

This book is not designed to be a textbook – it's designed to suggest to you various ways in which you can do some simple rearrangement of your family and business affairs in order to take advantage of the tax laws that will allow you to pass on more of your estate to your beneficiaries. When you have digested the contents of the book, you should decide what steps you feel comfortable about taking and you should then sit down with your financial advisor.

Do be careful and properly cautious but, equally, don't just put it all to one side. Action which is taken at an early stage is bound to yield more benefit than if you leave it until it is nearly too late altogether. It is worth the effort. Very few people wish the State to benefit at the expense of their family and significant improvements can often be achieved without doing anything complicated or giving away large sums of money.

This is particularly true of inheritance tax because it *can* be reduced by prudent and sensible planning. Indeed, as far as this tax is concerned, the taxman relies on our failure to make sound plans. Without some straightforward sensible planning, it's quite possible that a good proportion (and more than necessary) of *your* lifetimes efforts may go to the State rather than to your heirs. Of inheritance tax above all other taxes, it can truly be said that the taxman is the beneficiary of our inertia.

2 How the tax is calculated

Inheritance tax is a tricky subject . . .

The inheritance tax legislation is complicated. Most of the rules are contained in the Inheritance Tax Act 1984 which runs to 217 pages, and substantial parts of the last three Finance Acts were also devoted to this subject. In addition, there is a mass of Inland Revenue statements of practice, extra-statutory concessions. Some of the more obtuse aspects have even had to be clarified by the courts (we call this 'case law').

. . . but don't despair

Although the detailed workings of the tax can be bewildering, the main principles can be understood by a non-specialist. Let's begin by looking at the way that the tax is calculated. This is probably your first concern as you want to gauge the extent of the problem that could face your heirs after your death.

There are all manner of special rules which concern the way that certain assets such as shares in family companies and farmland are valued and you will need to refer to Chapter 8 which explains these rules. Those readers with more complex affairs will need to work through the book and then calculate (or 'compute') their potential liability by following the method set out in this chapter. However, perhaps we can leave these problems to one side for a moment and look at a fairly straightforward case.

The various steps are set out in the flow chart overleaf.

Let's work through the different steps one by one.

Your 'free estate'

This is merely the technical name for your net assets which belong to you absolutely. The term **free estate** is used because you are legally free to deal with this property in any way that you choose. This is to be contrasted with **settled property** where property is held for your benefit but you do not have absolute ownership and you have only limited rights over the capital.

Note that we are concerned only with *your* assets because those of your wife or husband will be dealt with separately for inheritance tax purposes.

People sometimes think that certain types of property that they own should not be counted as an asset. In practice however, almost every type of property does have to be included. Obvious items are things like:

- the open market value of your house or flat
- the house contents
- investment properties that you rent out
- stocks and shares
- unit trusts and similar investments
- money deposited at banks and building societies
- the balance standing to your credit on your current account.

Table 1: A straightforward computation

Husband   **Wife**

| Box 1 |
| Net value of |
| your free estate |
| £ |

↓ Add

| Box 2 |
| Value of settled |
| property |
| £ |

↓ Add

| Box 3 |
| Gifts which are |
| clawed back |
| £ |

↓ Add

| Box 4 |
| Chargeable transfers |
| made in last 7 years |
| £ |

↓ Deduct

| Box 5a |
| Property passing to |
| wife under your Will |
| £ |

↓ Add

| Box 5b |
| This property will |
| form part of husband's |
| estate when he dies |
| £ |

↓ Deduct

| Box 6 |
| Property left to charity |
| £ |

| Box 7 – net total |
| This is the figure |
| on which inheritance |
| tax is charged |
| £ |

| Box 1 |
| Net value of |
| your free estate |
| £ |

↓ Add

| Box 2 |
| Value of settled |
| property |
| £ |

↓ Add

| Box 3 |
| Gifts which are |
| clawed back |
| £ |

↓ Add

| Box 4 |
| Chargeable transfers |
| made in last 7 years |
| £ |

↓ Add

| Box 5a |
| This property will |
| form part of wife's |
| estate when she dies |
| £ |

↓ Deduct

| Box 5b |
| Property passing to |
| husband under your Will |
| £ |

↓ Deduct

| Box 6 |
| Property left to charity |
| £ |

| Box 7 – net total |
| This is the figure |
| on which inheritance |
| tax is charged. |
| £ |

Basically one takes the figure in Box 7, deducts the nil rate band (now £110,000) and the balance is charged at 40%. The tax actually payable may be less if the TOTAL of boxes 3 and 4 exceeds £110,000.

Less obvious for some people are:

- the value of any second home, whether this is in this country or overseas
- any property that you own and which is occupied by friends or relatives, even if they pay no rent
- the goodwill attaching to any business
- private loans to friends, relatives and family companies
- National Savings Certificates
- dividends which have been declared but not paid at the date of death
- interest on loans etc which has accrued up to that point in time
- the amount paid out on insurance policies owned by the deceased

In fact, the list is endless; most categories of property count and it is easier to say what need *not* be included:

- lump sums paid by a company pension scheme are usually exempt
- amounts paid over on insurance policies are exempt if the policy was 'written in trust' for someone else's benefit and therefore does not belong to the estate.

The figure to be included in Box 1 of Table 1 (see page 12) is the *net* value of your free estate, ie the difference between the total value of your capital and your debts. Almost everyone has some debts outstanding when they die if only because certain bills will not have been notified before the person died. Debts include things like:

- amount due on credit cards
- unpaid bills
- unpaid taxes (whether or not the actual amount had been assessed at the date of death)
- rates, ground rent, service charges etc, which were due up to the day that you died
- bank overdrafts
- bank loans

- money borrowed from friends and members of your family
- the amount owing on any mortgages.

The two main types of debts which *don't* normally qualify are:

1 Artificial debts, perhaps to a relative or friend, where the amounts due are higher than the value received. This is termed a debt which has not been incurred for valuable consideration.
2 Amounts borrowed from a person to whom you have made gifts.

Settled property

As mentioned already, property held in trust for your benefit is called 'settled property'. There are many different types of trust and the inheritance tax treatment varies accordingly. The general rule is that the capital value of any trust property is added to your free estate if you are entitled to receive the income of the trust as it arises. Similarly, if the trust owns a property which you are entitled to occupy rent-free, the value of that property has to be included. You are said to have an **'interest in possession'**.

Note that the value of the trust assets is included, not the value of your interest. A life interest in a trust owned by a person aged 100 might have only a small market value because of the limited life expectancy. Nevertheless, if the trust assets are worth £1 million it is that figure which has to be included in the beneficiary's estate because the life interest is an interest in possession.

If you are merely one of a class of potential beneficiaries and the trustees can pick and choose how they pay out the income, the above rules do not apply since you are not entitled to demand that the trustees should pay the income to you. This type of trust is called a **'discretionary trust'**.

If you are a beneficiary under a trust where someone else is entitled to the income, and you will benefit only on his death, you are said to have a **'reversionary interest'**. This does not form part of your estate unless you bought the interest from the person who was originally entitled to it.

Trusts can be very complicated (see Chapter 11). In practice it is sometimes difficult to determine which category a particular trust falls into and professional advice is desirable.

Gifts which are 'clawed back' for tax purposes

You might think that the answer is to give your property away before you die. However, things are not so simple as that. Certain property may have to be taken into account even though you have given it away:

- During the seven years leading up to your death (explained in more detail in the next chapter).
- Since 18 March 1986 but where you have retained the right to benefit from it ('gifts with reservation' which are also explained in the next chapter).

The inheritance tax treatment differs in each case. Of course, not everything you give away is taxed. There are certain exemptions.

Exemptions

The rules on exempt gifts need to be considered in relation to gifts made during the seven years preceding death, since it is only non-exempt gifts which are caught by the seven-year rule.

We have a chapter specifically devoted to this subject but in broad outline the following gifts are exempt:

- any gifts to a spouse (unless he or she is domiciled abroad – see Chapter 17)
- gifts not exceeding £250 per annum to any individual
- certain gifts 'in consideration of marriage'
- gifts to recognised charities and political parties
- the first £3,000 of any other gifts in any year.

Chargeable transfers made within seven years of death

Some transfers are treated as chargeable transfers right away, without waiting to see whether the donor dies within the seven year period. Such transfers can result in an immediate tax charge.

In practice, you will need to put something in Box 4 only if you made chargeable transfers before 18 March 1986 or created certain types of trust after that date. To begin with, transferring property to a trust was generally regarded as a chargeable transfer. The main exception was for gifts to a special type of accumulation and maintenance trust. Since 17 March 1987, chargeable transfers have occurred only when property is put into discretionary trust. See Chapter 3 for further details.

Exemptions on death

Not all property that passes to others on your death is liable to inheritance tax. The main exemptions which apply on death are the spouse exemption and property left to certain bodies.

There is usually an unlimited exemption for property which is left to your spouse or where your spouse becomes entitled to an interest in possession, eg your house is left in trust to your children but your spouse is entitled to live there rent-free.

In certain cases where your spouse is a foreign national, the exemption is not unlimited (see Chapter 17).

There is also an unlimited exemption for property left to a charity or a qualifying political party.

Working out the tax payable

This was formerly quite an involved business as inheritance tax rates varied from 30% to 60%. Now it is relatively straightforward: the first £110,000 of chargeable transfers attract inheritance tax at 0% (this is called the 'nil rate band'). The excess is charged at a flat rate of 40%.

Taper relief on gifts

It seems unfair that a gift is caught if the donor dies six years and 364 days after making the gift but is ignored altogether if he survives seven years. If this rule applied rigidly the death of the donor one minute before midnight could cost the recipient 40%! To avoid this unfair result the legislation allows taper relief so that the inheritance tax is reduced if the donor survives at least three years.

The relief reduces the tax otherwise payable as follows:

If the donor survives	*Reduction*
three complete years	20%
four complete years	40%
five complete years	60%
six complete years	80%

EXAMPLE

A gift of £200,000 made six years ago becomes chargeable when the donor dies. The inheritance tax would normally be £36,000. This is reduced by taper relief of 80% so that only £7,200 is actually payable.

Who pays the tax?

If you have made any gifts which are caught by the seven year rule, it is the person who received the gift (the 'donee') who is liable to pay any inheritance tax which becomes due. On the other hand, the nil rate band is allocated to these gifts before it is set against your estate so the tax payable by the donees may be less than you would expect. The real impact may be borne by your executors.

EXAMPLE

Alan dies in 1989 and leaves a free estate of £480,000. If this had been the end of the story, the inheritance tax payable by the executors would have been £148,000, (£480,000 less the £110,000 nil rate band × 40%). However, it transpires that he gave his son £120,000 in 1987. Because this falls within the seven-year period the total inheritance tax is calculated thus:

Gifts 'caught' by seven-year rule	£120,000
Free estate	480,000
	600,000
less nil rate band	110,000
Taxable	490,000

and the inheritance tax is £196,000.

However, this is not divided evenly. The tax payable by the son is calculated as:

Amount of gift	£120,000
less nil rate band	110,000
Taxable	10,000

and the son would be responsible for tax of £4,000, leaving the executors with a liability for £192,000.

The effect of this rule needs to be borne in mind when a person wishes to treat his offspring equally. Suppose Alan had four daughters as well as his son and he had left his free estate to his daughters since he had already provided for his son. In a sense, he gave or left all five of his children £120,000. However, because of the way in which the rules operate, the son got £116,000 whereas the daughters received only £56,000 after tax.

Where there is settled property

If settled property is involved, the total inheritance tax is divided on a proportionate basis.

EXAMPLE

Brian leaves free estate of	£140,000
He is entitled to an interest in possession in settled property worth	460,000
	£600,000

Inheritance tax is charged as follows:	600,000
less nil rate band	110,000
	£490,000
Tax at 40% thereon	£196,000

This is divided:

payable by executors $\dfrac{140,000}{600,000}$ ×   £196,000   =   £45,733

payable by trustees $\dfrac{460,000}{600,000}$ ×   £196,000   =   £150,267

3 How gifts are treated

Gifts can be a very effective way of avoiding inheritance tax provided that such gifts are made in a properly planned way. On the other hand, there are pitfalls to be avoided. Chapter 11 deals with the main principles of 'the art of gifting', but before we can go into the possibilities for saving tax we need to explain the tax treatment of lifetime transfers in greater detail. The flow chart at the end of the chapter will help you to work out the way in which gifts made by you will be treated.

Exempt and potentially exempt transfers

A key distinction that we have not previously mentioned is that between 'exempt' and *'potentially* exempt' transfers. A gift which is covered by one of the specific exemptions is exempt immediately so that it is left out of account even if the donor dies the very next day. A potentially exempt transfer or 'PET' is potentially exempt because it will not be counted for IHT purposes if the donor survives the seven-year period. If and when the donor survives that period the potentially exempt transfer becomes actually exempt but if he dies in that period the gift becomes a chargeable transfer.

Certain gifts are not potentially exempt at all, ie they do not even have the potential to become exempt. Gifts with reservation where the donor retains a benefit (see Chapter 4) are effectively disregarded and the property remains part of the donor's estate even if he survives the seven-year period.

Why do we refer to transfers rather than 'gifts'?

It is impossible to avoid jargon if we are to accurately summarise the law. All gifts are transfers but not all transfers are gifts. It may not be right technically to say that a person who knowingly sells his son a yacht worth £100,000 for £60,000 is making a gift but he is certainly making a transfer of value of £40,000. Deliberately omitting to exercise a right can also be a transfer of value, but this is not a gift in the normal sense of the word. Also a transfer can involve property that is not owned by the person such as where a person renounces an entitlement to income under a trust.

EXAMPLE

Claude is entitled to all the income arising from a family settlement worth £1.5 million. If he died this would count as part of his estate because he has an interest in possession in the trust. He renounces his entitlement so that it will no longer be included. He is regarded as making a transfer of value of £1.5 million.

There must be 'gratuitous intent'

Don't worry, the Inland Revenue can't assess a bad bargain as a transfer of value. There must be gratuitous intent, ie an intention on your part to make a gift. Of course, the burden of proof may rest with you (or your executors): if you sold an asset to a close relative at a knockdown price they may have to produce evidence in order to demonstrate that this was not a disguised gift.

How a transfer is measured

Another thing to be borne in mind is that the amount of the transfer may be determined by the reduction in the donor's worth. This is not necessarily the same as the increase in the recipient's wealth.

Once again this is best illustrated by an example. A person who owns 51 out of the 100 shares in a company has control. Perhaps the shares that he owns are worth £2,000 each, ie £102,000 in total. If he gives two shares to his son he relinquishes control of the company and an outsider might only be prepared to pay £50,000 to acquire his remaining 49 shares. The two shares may not be worth very much in isolation and the son may not have acquired a very valuable asset, but the father's estate has gone down in value by £52,000. It is this figure which is taken as the transfer of value.

Certain gifts are not transfers of value

The proper procedure is to ascertain the amount of the transfer of value then deduct any exemption. What is left is either a potentially exempt transfer or a chargeable transfer. However, some transactions never get this far. For example, payments for the maintenance of dependants are not treated as transfers of value in the first place.

Maintenance of dependants, family etc

The legislation specifically provides that the following lifetime payments are not transfers of value:

- payments for the maintenance of a spouse or former spouse

- payments for the maintenance, education or training of a child or step-child under the age of 18
- payments made to maintain a child over 18 who is in full-time education or training
- reasonable provision for the care or maintenance of a dependent relative, ie someone who is incapacitated by old age or infirmity from maintaining himself, or a widowed, separated or divorced mother or mother-in-law.

Waivers of dividends

Waivers of dividends or remuneration may also not be regarded as transfers of value. In practice these normally arise only in a family company situation and we can, therefore, leave them until we look at family companies in greater depth in Chapter 8.

There is another type of transaction which is specifically excluded from the definition of a transfer of value and, which is much more common. As it is more frequently encountered we will now look at the rules governing interest-free loans.

Interest-free loans

Where a person makes an interest-free loan, the gift is the interest that the person might have charged, ie the interest he or she has 'foregone'. The inheritance tax legislation provides that an interest-free loan is not to be treated as a transfer of value provided that the loan is repayable upon demand. If the loan is made for a specific period, and the lender has no legal right to call for repayment before that time, the grant of the loan could be a transfer of value and this aspect needs to be carefully considered. In such a case the transfer would be measured by the difference between the amount of the loan and the market value of the right to receive payment in, say, ten or 15 years' time.

Exempt gifts

The full list of exempt gifts is as follows:

- gifts to spouse
- normal expenditure out of income
- £250 small gifts exemption
- annual £3,000 exemption
- exemption for marriage gifts
- gifts to charities
- gifts for national purposes
- gifts for public benefit
- gifts to political parties.

It is worth looking in closer detail at the conditions which need to be satisfied.

Spouse exemption

There is normally an unlimited exemption for gifts between husband and wife. There may be a limit of £55,000 if one of you (the recipient) has a foreign domicile. In practice, this is most likely to apply if one of you is a foreign national and we will explain how the restriction works in Chapter 17.

Normal expenditure out of income

A lifetime gift is exempt if it is shown that the gift was made as part of the normal expenditure of the donor and comes out of income. In theory, it needs to be demonstrated that the gift was typical or habitual and that if one looks at a period of several years the pattern of such gifts has left the donor with sufficient income to maintain his normal standard of living. In practice, the Revenue do not disputed regular gifts of modest size.

Certain types of income must be excluded when looking at the donor's net income. In particular, it is necessary to exclude the capital element of annuities purchased after 12 November 1974.

In the past this exemption has often been overlooked, but now that income tax rates have fallen and people have more spendable income, it may be much more important.

Small gifts exemption

Gifts of up to £250 to any particular person in any one tax year are exempt. Where the gift to any individual exceeds £250 the exemption is lost completely.

Once again, the potential of utilising this exemption has often been overlooked. You may well have three children who between them have acquired three wives and produced ten grandchildren. If you were so minded you and your wife could each make exempt gifts totalling £4,000 each tax year.

Annual exemption

Gifts of £3,000 are exempt each year and both husband and wife have separate annual exemptions unlike, for instance, capital gains tax where there is a joint annual exemption. The £3,000 can be set against part of larger gifts, ie if you give four sons £10,000 and you have not used your £3,000 allowance, then £3,000 is exempt and the balance is a PET. If the full £3,000 is not used in a given year the balance can be carried forward for *one year only* and is then allowable only when the exemption for that second year is fully utilised.

EXAMPLE 1

Gifts made in year 1		£1,000
Balance of exemption carried to year 2		2,000
Gifts made in year 2		4,000
Annual exemption for year 2	3,000	
Part of unused exemption for year 1	1,000	4,000
Chargeable gifts		Nil

The balance of exemption from year 1 of £1,000 may *not* be carried forward to year 3.

EXAMPLE 2

Year 1 as in Example 1 – unused exemption	£2,000
Exemption for year 2	£3,000
Year 2 gifts	2,000
Balance of year 2 exemption to be carried forward to year 3	£1,000

The balance of the year 1 exemption of £2,000 may *not* be carried forward to year 3.

The exemption is used first against chargeable lifetime gifts, ie those not potentially exempt and any balance is then available to be set against PETs made in that year which subsequently become chargeable because the donor dies within the next 7 years.

Gifts in consideration of marriage

Gifts made to the bride or groom in consideration of their marriage are exempt as shown in Table 2.

Table 2: Gifts in consideration of marriage

Gifts made by	*Maximum exemption*
each parent	£5,000
grandparents	£2,500
bride or groom	£2,500
any other person	£1,000

It should be noted that parents may make gifts to either party to the marriage – their exemption is not restricted to gifts made to their own child provided that the sum of the gifts made by each parent does not exceed £5,000.

Once again the exemption can be used to cover part of a larger gift.

Gifts to charities

Gifts to charities which are established in the UK are exempt regardless of the amount. A charity may be established or 'registered' here even though it carries out its work overseas and the exemption covers gifts to such charities. Donations made to a charity established abroad do not normally qualify.

Gifts for national purposes

Gifts to certain national bodies are totally exempt. These bodies include the National Trust, colleges and universities, the National Gallery, the British Museum and other galleries and museums run by local authorities or universities.

Gifts for public benefit

It is necessary to clear the position in advance with HM Treasury if this exemption is to be available. It covers gifts of eligible property such as historic buildings, land of outstanding scenic, historic or scientific interest, works of art and collections of national scientific, historic or artistic interest.

Gifts to political parties

Gifts to qualifying political parties are only exempt if certain conditions are satisfied. A political party qualifies if it had at least two members of parliament returned at the last general election, or if it had at least one member and more than 150,000 votes were cast for its candidates.

Immediately chargeable transfers

Not all transfers are capable of being PETs. The main exception is where a person transfers property into a **discretionary trust** (see Chapter 11). Such a transfer is treated as a chargeable transfer and inheritance tax is payable immediately at half of the rate applicable on death.

EXAMPLE

Daphne decides to set up a discretionary trust for the benefit of her adult nephews and nieces. She transfers securities worth £150,000 to the trust. This is neither an exempt, nor a potentially exempt, transfer. In fact, it is a chargeable transfer and inheritance tax is charged on the following basis:

Chargeable transfers in previous seven years	nil
Value transferred	150,000
	150,000
less nil rate band	110,000
Taxable	40,000
Tax thereon at 20%	£8,000

If Daphne had previously made other chargeable transfers of, say, £50,000, the computation would have been:

Chargeable transfers in previous seven years	50,000
Value transferred	150,000
	200,000
less nil rate band	110,000
Taxable	90,000
Tax thereon at 20%	£18,000

If the previous chargeable transfers had exceeded the nil rate band, the whole amount of the chargeable transfer would have attracted inheritance tax at 20%.

If the person dies within three years of making a chargeable transfer the rate of tax is increased from 50% to 100% of the normal rate. Thus, if Daphne died two years after setting up the trust the tax would be charged at 40% rather than 20%.

Conditions for a transfer to be a PET

As we have already mentioned a potentially exempt transfer is a transfer which is exempt once you have lived for seven years. However, not all gifts can count as PETs. A potentially exempt transfer can only consist of one of the following:

- an outright gift to an individual
- a transfer to a trust under which an individual has an interest in possession
- a transfer to an accumulation and maintenance trust (see Chapter 11).

A PET must also come outside the rules governing gifts with reservation (which are fully defined in Chapter 4).

Tax charged on a PET because of death within seven years

We have already looked at the way in which extra inheritance tax may be charged on the estate because of death within the seven year period. It is now necessary to look more closely at the way that tax is charged on the PET itself.

The tax charge on the transfer which has turned out not to be exempt is computed on the following basis. For the purposes of valuation, the transfer is treated as a chargeable transfer made at the time it was made, but with the liability being calculated by using the rates in force at the date of death.

More complicated cases

So far we have looked only at the most straightforward case where the PET 'stands alone' and was not preceded by any chargeable transfers. The position becomes more complex where there were chargeable transfers in the seven years before the PET occurred (and the rules which governed whether a transfer was a chargeable transfer were changed on 18 March 1986). In these cases, you should seek professional advice.

Benefits of making PETs

PETs are currently treated favourably in that the scale of rates that are used are those in force at death, which can be nearly seven years later. However, don't forget that rates could rise.

Another way in which PETs are treated favourably is that the value is fixed by the value transferred. Even if the property appreciates in value the increase in value still escapes a charge to inheritance tax on the donor's death.

Thus, if a person made a gift of property worth £200,000 in August 1986 and he dies in June 1988, the inheritance tax would be:

Value transferred	£200,000
Less nil rate band	110,000
	90,000
Inheritance tax at 40%	£36,000

It is irrelevant that the property was worth, say, £350,000 at the date of death.

Position if property goes down in value

The legislation provides that inheritance tax shall be charged on the value at the time that the PET was made or at the time of death, *whichever is the less*. This rule has been very useful in dealing with situations which have arisen since October 1987.

EXAMPLE

In July 1987 Aunt Agatha gave her favourite nephew a portfolio of shares. They were then worth £200,000. When she died in November 1987 after the crash the shares were worth only £100,000. The top rate of inheritance tax at that time was 60% so if no relief were available the nephew could have ended up out of pocket. Fortunately, the inheritance tax on the gift can be calculated on £100,000 rather than the original £200,000.

The points covered in this chapter can also be followed by working through the flowchart below.

Table 3: Chargeable or exempt transfer?

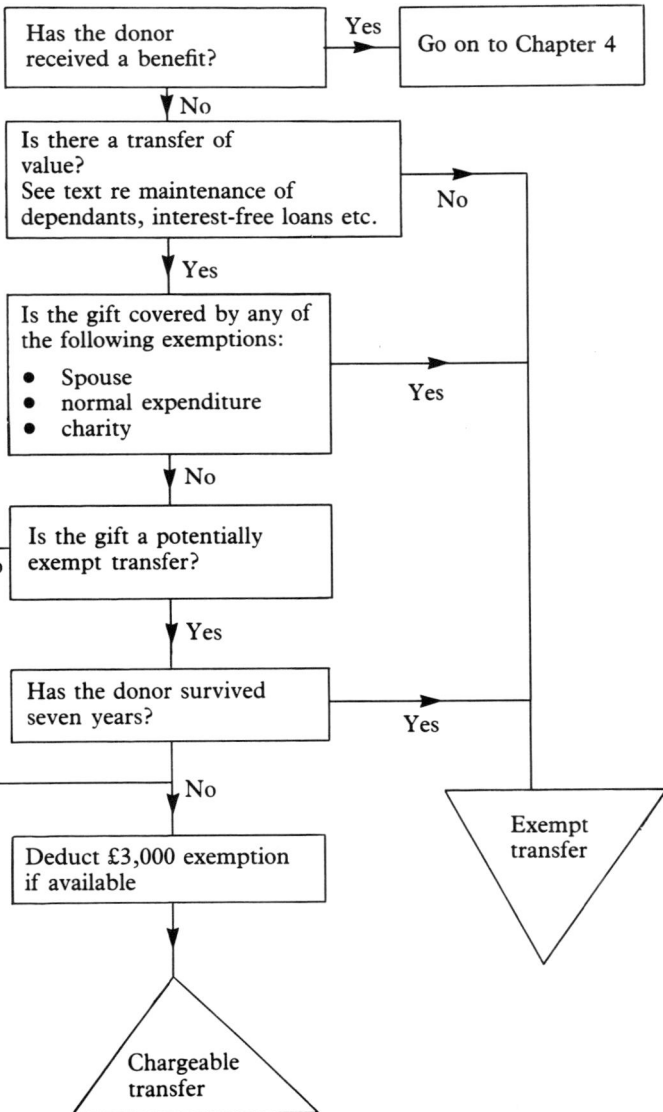

Has the donor received a benefit?	**Yes** → Go on to Chapter 4

No ↓

Is there a transfer of value?
See text re maintenance of dependants, interest-free loans etc. — **No** →

Yes ↓

Is the gift covered by any of the following exemptions:
- Spouse
- normal expenditure
- charity

Yes →

No ↓

Is the gift a potentially exempt transfer? — **No**

Yes ↓

Has the donor survived seven years? — **Yes** →

No ↓

Deduct £3,000 exemption if available

↓

Chargeable transfer

Exempt transfer

4 Gifts with reservation: gifts the taxman disallows

In March 1986 the rules were changed to enable the Revenue to ignore **'gifts with reservation'**. In practice, many people want to do precisely what the rule is intended to prevent, ie give away the *capital* value of an asset but retain either the *income* to cover their living expenses, or the right to get the *capital* itself back should their circumstances change. Before 18 March 1986 many people did just this by making use of inheritance trust and discounted gift schemes devised by insurance companies. The publicity given to these schemes led the Government to go to the other extreme and introduce this rule. Gifts made before the law was changed are not, in general, affected.

Two-pronged test

The actual words of the legislation say that property which is gifted after 17 March 1986 may still be regarded as forming part of a person's estate unless:

(a) possession and enjoyment of the property was bona fide assumed by the donee, and

(b) the property is enjoyed to the entire exclusion, or virtually to the entire exclusion, of the donor and of any benefit to him or her by contract or otherwise

It is easy enough to think of gifts which would fail to satisfy the first test, an obvious example would be a gift of a house which the donor continued to occupy. The second test would catch the situation where the donor moved out but came back later on.

The legislation does actually say that the property must be enjoyed 'to the entire exclusion, *or virtually to the entire exclusion* of the donor'. However, in practice it is prudent to regard this as if it excludes *all* benefit to the donor, no matter how small. The Inland Revenue's view is that the exception is intended to cover trivial benefits such as might arise where the donor of a picture enjoyed the chance to view it when making occasional visits to the donee's home.

The legislation also refers to a benefit reserved 'by contract *or otherwise*'. This refers to arrangements which are not legally binding but which amount to some sort of 'understanding'. For example, there could be a reserved benefit where a person gives away a painting or a fur coat on the understanding that he or she can borrow it from time to time even though the donor had no legally enforceable rights.

Benefits enjoyed by the spouse of a donor do not constitute a benefit to the donor and, therefore, do not normally affect the validity of the gift. However the Revenue may well attack a situation where the spouse passes money straight on to the donor.

Two specific exceptions

The legislation specifically states that occupation of property or use of chattels (furniture, paintings etc) does not count as a benefit *provided* a market rent is paid. It also says that a benefit enjoyed by a donor occupying property can be ignored in a case where the donor's financial circumstances have changed drastically for the worse after the gift has been made. However, the Inland Revenue are bound to require firm evidence before agreeing that either of these let-outs apply.

Interpreting this rule

In a way this rule was not a completely new concept as a similar rule applied for estate duty before it was replaced by capital transfer tax in March 1974. The actual words of the legislation are virtually identical to those which applied to estate duty and there is a considerable number of decided cases which show how the courts interpret the rule in borderline circumstances.

This case law is especially relevant where a gift to a trust is contemplated. Unfortunately, the way in which the rule applies is surprisingly harsh in that a benefit is regarded as having been reserved unless the donor is totally excluded from any *possible* benefit. This means, for example, that a gift to a discretionary trust may be caught if the donor is one of the class of potential beneficiaries or if his name can be added to such a class later on. We will go into this in greater detail in Chapter 18.

Position where reservation of benefit ceases

Where a person makes a gift and reserves a benefit and that benefit is then relinquished, the donor is treated as making a potentially exempt transfer at the time that he gives up the benefit. The amount of the PET is governed by the market value of the property at that time.

EXAMPLE

Ernest Hopeful decides to give the family estate to his son. When he made the gift in 1987 it was worth £200,000. However, Ernest reserves a benefit by continuing to live there rent-free until 1990 when he moves out. The estate is then worth £400,000. In 1996 Ernest dies.

In 1987 the gift would be disallowed as a gift with reservation. In 1990, when that reserved benefit ceased, Ernest would be treated as making a potentially exempt transfer of property worth £400,000.

This notional PET is caught because he dies within the seven year period. Had Ernest not reserved a benefit the PET would have been made in 1987 and would be exempt under the seven year rule by the time Ernest died in 1996.

The gift with reservation rule does not apply to gifts which are covered by the following exemptions:

- small gifts
- gifts to spouse
- gifts in consideration of marriage
- gifts to charity
- gifts for national purposes
- gifts for public benefit
- gifts to political parties.

This chapter has involved some complicated rules and the flowchart overleaf should help in identifying the key aspects.

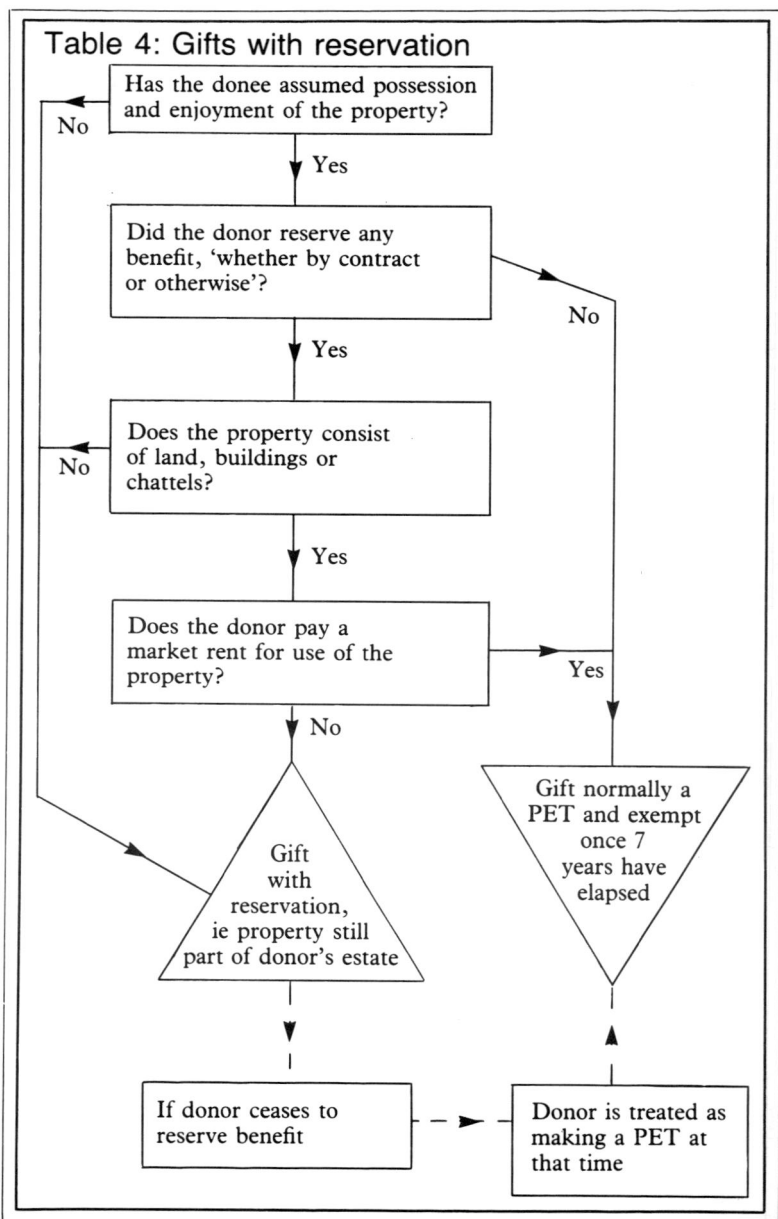

Table 4: Gifts with reservation

Has the donee assumed possession and enjoyment of the property?

No

↓ Yes

Did the donor reserve any benefit, 'whether by contract or otherwise'?

No

↓ Yes

Does the property consist of land, buildings or chattels?

No

↓ Yes

Does the donor pay a market rent for use of the property?

Yes

↓ No

Gift with reservation, ie property still part of donor's estate

Gift normally a PET and exempt once 7 years have elapsed

If donor ceases to reserve benefit -- ➤ Donor is treated as making a PET at that time

5 Your position as a beneficiary of a trust

In Chapter 2, we briefly outlined the way in which the capital value of certain trusts may have to be added to your personal property or 'free estate'. It is now appropriate to take a closer look at the various types of trust and the way that beneficiaries are treated.

Trusts may be created by a lifetime gift or come into being through the provisions of a Will. The responsibilities and duties of trustees and the rights of beneficiaries are normally set out in a legal document or 'trust deed'. There are basically five main types of trust for inheritance tax purposes:

- exempt pre-13 November 1974 Will trusts
- other interest in possession trusts
- discretionary trusts
- accumulation and maintenance trusts
- foreign trusts.

Let's go through these in turn:

Exempt pre-13 November 1974 Will trusts

This section will only be relevant to a person who benefits under a trust created by the Will of a person who died before 13 November 1974 and left property in trust on the following terms:

- his or her surviving spouse is entitled to an interest in possession

- the surviving spouse must not be entitled to demand that capital be paid out to him or her.

These are a special type of interest in possession trust. An **interest in possession** exists where the beneficiary is entitled to income arising from the trust capital and is legally entitled to demand that the trustees pay that income to him or her. An interest in possession can also exist where the trust owns a property and the beneficiary is entitled to live there rent free.

Typically these type of trusts give a widow (or widower) the right to income during her (or his) lifetime, with the property then passing to other beneficiaries, eg children, on the death of the widow (or widower). The widow (or widower) is called a life tenant. Those people who will benefit on his or her death are called **reversionary beneficiaries** because the trust property reverts to them when the widow's (or widowers) life interest comes to an end.

Some further clarification is required.

A Will trust qualifies for exemption only if the beneficiary has no power to demand capital. This does not mean that the terms of the trust must prohibit such payments but it does mean that the power or discretion to pay out capital lies with the trustees and the beneficiary cannot insist that they do so.

These trusts are exempt because before 13 November 1974 estate duty was levied on the death of the spouse. No inheritance tax is payable on the death of the surviving spouse who has an interest in possession, nor is the value of the trust capital aggregated with his or her free estate.

Will trusts which came into being after 12 November 1974 are treated differently because of the exemption which now applies for property passing to a surviving spouse. For estate duty a charge was levied on the free estate but not on the death of the surviving spouse, for capital transfer tax and inheritance tax it is the other way round. Either way the property is charged once and only once.

If you have a reversionary interest in such a trust, ie you expect to inherit the capital at some time in the future, it does not normally count as part of your estate. This means that inheritance tax is not charged if you die before the life tenant. Also, you can make an exempt gift by assigning your entitlement to your children or other heirs. The only exception to this rule is if you purchased your reversionary interests from someone else.

Other interest in possession trusts

Exempt pre 13 November 1974 trusts are merely one special type of interest in possession trusts. Basically, a trust falls into this general classification if the trust provides that one or more beneficiaries have an interest in possession. As we have seen, such a beneficiary is called a life tenant. The capital value of the trust property is aggregated with the life tenant's 'free estate' on death (see Chapter 2).

If you are the life tenant and decide that you can make do without the income, you can **renounce your entitlement**. You are then treated as making a PET equal to the value of the net trust assets. Inheritance tax is payable in the normal way if you die within seven years and must be paid by the trustees or the people who have taken the trust property if the trust has been wound up.

If you have a reversionary interest in such a trust it does not normally count as part of your estate. It is said to be 'excluded property'. This means that inheritance tax is not charged if you die before the life tenant. Also, you can make an exempt gift by assigning your entitlement to your children or other heirs. The only exception to this rule is if you purchased your reversionary interest from someone else.

Discretionary trusts

This is a type of trust where the trustees do not have to pay the income to a particular beneficiary but can 'pick and choose' as to how they allocate income to members of a class of potential beneficiaries. Very often the class of such beneficiaries is restricted to a small group of relatives such as the children and grandchildren of the person who created the trust (known as the **'settlor'**).

Some trust deeds permit the trustees to accumulate income, in other words to re-invest income rather than pay it out to a beneficiary. It is also common for the trustees to have power to distribute capital so that investments and other capital may be realised and the proceeds paid over to a particular beneficiary.

If you are a beneficiary of such a trust you can rest easy. There is no charge on the trust property upon your death unless an appointment has been made to you and then it becomes part of your estate. If the trustees distribute capital to you they may have to pay inheritance tax (this is called the **'exit charge'**). Normally this arises only where the trust is substantial, ie worth more than £110,000. The absolute maximum rate of tax is 6%.

The trustees may also be subject to a **'periodic charge'** every ten years, with the trustees being assessed at 6% on the extent to which the trust investments exceed the nil rate band.

Accumulation and maintenance trusts

An accumulation and maintenance trust is a special type of discretionary trust where the discretion left to the trustees is much reduced. In general, for a trust to qualify as an accumulation and maintenance trust, the deed must specify that the prime beneficiaries are a class of people aged below 25. Furthermore, the trust must provide that at least one or more members of this class must become entitled to an interest in possession no later than their 25th birthdays.

The trustees can still have some discretion. For example, they can accumulate or pay out income arising whilst the beneficiaries are minors. The deed may allow them a choice so that they can choose to exclude a particular beneficiary, but if they do this the effect must be that some other beneficiaries who are aged below 25 will receive an interest in possession when they attain that age. The deed can provide for capital etc to pass to some other beneficiary if all the prime beneficiaries die under 25, but this is the only circumstance which can be permitted. Apart from this possibility, the deed must provide that a beneficiary will take an interest in possession on attaining that age (or before).

Accumulation and maintenance trusts are favourably treated. The periodic charge mentioned above does not apply. Also, there is no exit charge. If a beneficiary dies after he has become entitled to an interest in possession which, as we have said, must be no later than age 25, the relevant proportion of the trust property is treated as forming part of his estate.

Once all the beneficiaries have obtained an interest in possession of the relevant proportion of the trust property, the trust ceases to be an accumulation and maintenance trust and becomes a straight forward interest in possession trust.

Foreign trusts

There is a special category of trusts which are created by a person of foreign domicile (see Chapter 11). Such a trust can be an interest in possession trust, a discretionary trust or any other kind of trust. In so far as the trustees own property in the UK, it is treated in the same way as other trusts of the same type. However, no inheritance tax liability arises in respect of foreign property owned by the trust since the foreign property is said to be 'excluded property'.

The flowchart opposite summerises the main principles.

Table 5: Position of beneficiary

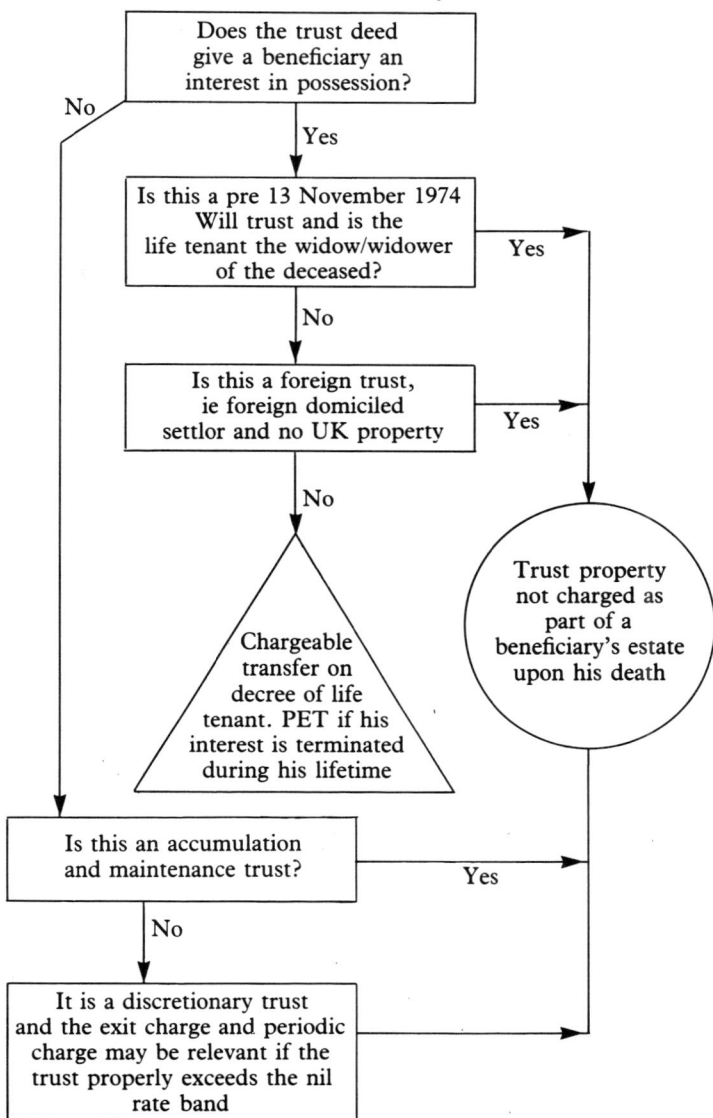

Does the trust deed
give a beneficiary an
interest in possession?

No

Yes

Is this a pre 13 November 1974
Will trust and is the
life tenant the widow/widower
of the deceased?

Yes

No

Is this a foreign trust,
ie foreign domiciled
settlor and no UK property

Yes

No

Chargeable
transfer on
decree of life
tenant. PET if his
interest is terminated
during his lifetime

Trust property
not charged as
part of a
beneficiary's estate
upon his death

Is this an accumulation
and maintenance trust?

Yes

No

It is a discretionary trust
and the exit charge and periodic
charge may be relevant if the
trust properly exceeds the nil
rate band

6 What happens if you don't make a Will?

In this chapter we start by looking at the consequences and inheritance tax implications of dying intestate, ie if you die without making a valid Will. We then look at some common types of Will and their tax consequences.

Intestacy

The law in Scotland is different (see letigim in Chapter 16), but in England and Wales the following rules apply if a person dies without leaving a Will.

Surviving spouse (but no children)

All the personal **chattels** (furniture, clothes, car etc) go to the surviving spouse. He or she is also entitled to the first *£125,000* of the rest of the estate. The survivor will also be entitled to a *half of the residue* with the other half passing to the deceased's parents or (if the parents have died) to brothers or sisters or their children. If the survivor wishes he or she may take the matrimonial home as part of the half share.

Surviving spouse and surviving children

The spouse is entitled to the deceased's chattels and the first £75,000. He or she then gets a **life interest** in one-half of the residue. The remaining half passes to the children immediately. When the surviving spouse dies, the children also receive the capital from the property which was held in trust during the lifetime of the surviving spouse.

No surviving spouse but surviving children

If a person leaves children the estate is divided equally between them. If one of the children has died already, his or her children normally take the amount to which their parent would have been entitled.

No surviving spouse and no surviving children

Where there are no children, the estate passes to the parents if they are alive. If they are not, the estate passes to any brothers or sisters, and then on to their children. If this still does not produce an heir, the estate passes to any surviving grandparents or failing this will go to any aunts or uncles. If this fails to find an heir, the property passes to the Crown.

It is significant that *common-law* wives and husbands obtain no benefit under the intestacy rules, although they can apply to the court for 'reasonable provision'.

Inheritance tax implications

The main consequence of dying intestate is that inheritance tax will be payable, unless the amount which does not pass to your spouse is below the nil rate band. However, there may be circumstances where tax is payable even though less than £110,000 passes to your children or parents on your death. This may apply where either:

- you are the life tenant of a family trust

- you have made substantial gifts within the last seven years
- where you have made gifts that are caught because you reserved benefit.

EXAMPLE

Fred dies in 1989 without making a Will. He left a wife and an adult daughter from a former marriage. At one time he had been very well off but his business interests failed in 1986 and he left an estate worth £200,000 made up as follows:

House	140,000
Personal effects (chattels)	30,000
Cash and securities	30,000
	£200,000

The widow and daughter don't get on.

His widow is entitled to the personal effects and to property worth £75,000 and a life interest in half of what is left, which amounts to £47,500. The total of the widow's entitlement is therefore £152,500. The other £47,500 passes to the daughter. That is the first problem as the estate does not have property which can be readily realised to pay out £47,500 to the daughter.

It then transpires that Fred had made a gift of £50,000 to his parents in 1983 before his business got into difficulties and that he was the life tenant of a family trust worth £100,000 where the trust property passed to his brother on Fred's death. This could result in inheritance tax being payable as follows:

Free estate	200,000
Settled property	100,000
Gift within seven years	50,000
	350,000
Less exempt (because it passes to Fred's wife)	152,500
	£197,500
Inheritance tax thereon	£35,000

This would be divided proportionately between the daughter (who has £47,500) and the trust (which has £100,000). This means that the daughter would have inheritance tax of nearly £12,000 deducted from her £47,500.

Personal implications

Resentment and arguments about money can bring out the worst in some people, especially if relationships are strained already. It is highly unlikely that the intestacy rules will result in your possessions being distributed as you would wish. Even if they did, it would still be better to make a Will as this deals with the position 'more cleanly' and enables the estate to be administered more promptly and with less bother and expense.

We will go into the practical aspects of making a Will in Chapter 9. The rest of this chapter is concerned with the inheritance tax implications of some of the more common ways in which Wills are drawn up.

Spouse as the main beneficiary

Many Wills, indeed the vast majority, consist of a few minor bequests and provisions leaving almost all the estate to the deceased's spouse. The Will may refer to the 'residue' that means all that is left after the specific bequests have been declared.

There are variations on a theme, eg some people name their spouse as the beneficiary provided she or he survives a period of one month. Some people even specify that the spouse must survive six months if she or he is to take the residue. Wills are often drafted this way in case husband and wife are both involved in an accident. These variations don't normally make a lot of difference from a tax point of view. Property which passes to a spouse is exempt whether she or he gets it right away or only on satisfying such a survivorship requirement. The only limitation is that six months is the longest period that may be specified.

Property left in trust for spouse

Some people leave part or all of their property in trust so that their spouse is entitled to the income or benefit during his or her lifetime but is not entitled to the capital. On the death of the spouse the property then passes to other beneficiaries as set out in the Will. A common provision is to leave property in trust for a widow with the property being divided on her death among the children of the marriage in equal shares.

Once again, property which is left in trust in this way is exempt since the surviving spouse has an interest in possession. Inheritance tax will, of course, normally be charged on the spouse's subsequent death.

Property left to parents, children, grandchildren etc

These legacies are not exempt and inheritance tax will be payable if they exceed what is left of the nil rate band.

Property left to charities

These legacies are normally exempt.

Property left subject to discretionary trusts

Some Wills are drawn up so that the executors may distribute capital at their discretion to any one of a range or 'class' of potential beneficiaries. The class might, for example, include the spouse, children, grandchildren etc. People include such provisions in their Will because they recognise that there may be certain needs and requirements which they cannot foresee. Quite often the executors include the widow or widower and professional advisers with whom the deceased has discussed his wishes as to how they should deal with the property in certain circumstances.

The tax treatment depends upon whether the executors or trustees distribute capital within two years of the death. If they do this the capital paid out is treated as if it passed in the deceased's Will and the inheritance tax on his death is worked out on that basis. No inheritance tax is payable if capital is distributed to the spouse within this period as the capital is treated in the same way as if it had been left to the spouse outright. If property remains in trust at the end of the two year period, this benefit falls away and the inheritance tax is computed in the usual way. There may also be an 'exit charge' if the trustees subsequently decide to distribute capital (see Chapter 5 on discretionary trusts).

A mixture of all these?

The provisions above are not mutually exclusive and many Wills contain more than one of them.

Action which can be taken after a person has died

So far we have considered the ways in which writing a Will can improve the overall inheritance tax position. It is also possible to take some action after a person has died to reduce the impact of inheritance tax.

Disclaiming legacies

A person has become entitled to property under a Will or a trust may disclaim his or her entitlement particularly if his children benefit as a result. You may also disclaim an entitlement under the intestacy provisions. A **disclaimer** means that you give up your entitlement, it does not permit you to direct that someone else should stand in your stead. This may be achieved through a deed of variation (see below).

Such a disclaimer is normally effective for tax purposes provided that:

- no payment or other consideration is given for the disclaimer
- the person has not already accepted his entitlement, either 'expressly or by implication' (see below).

The tax legislation does not say much beyond this. Difficulties in knowing whether a disclaimer is effective arise from the way that trust law operates in general rather than from the inheritance tax legislation. Expressly accepting a legacy or other entitlement would apply where the person had started to assume some benefit. In any event any delay between becoming entitled and disclaiming might constitute accepting it 'by implication' and such delays should be avoided. Obviously you should take legal advice before disclaiming a legacy. Particular care concerning the legal formalities is required where a person wishes to disclaim only part of a legacy, since this may involve a deed of variation.

Deeds of variation

These are sometimes called 'deeds of family arrangement'. They differ from disclaimers in that they relate only to property which belonged to the person who has died and not to settled property which forms part of his estate for tax purposes. Also, the effect of a person entering into a deed of variation may be to re-direct property to a particular person whereas a person making a disclaimer simply gives up his entitlement.

The deed of variation must be executed within two years of the death and an election must be filed within six months.

The revised manner in which the deceased person's property is distributed is then treated as if it had flowed from the deceased person's Will. In other words the parties to the deed effectively re-write the deceased person's Will. They are not treated as making any transfers, the re-distribution is treated as if it occurred on the occasion of the death.

EXAMPLE

Aubrey died in January 1988 leaving his entire estate to his wife. She is herself elderly and very well off in her own right. A deed of variation could be entered into so that chargeable transfers would arise on Aubrey's death which would make use of his nil rate band (at that time, £90,000). For example, property worth that amount could pass to their children. Although the wife would be giving up an entitlement, she would not be treated as making a capital transfer.

Conditions which need to be satisfied

Certain conditions need to be satisfied:

1 The deed must be in writing and specifically refer to the provisions of the Will etc which are to be varied.
2 It must be signed by the person who would otherwise have benefited and anybody else who might have benefited.
3 Only one deed of variation in respect of a piece of property can be effective for tax purposes so it is vitally important to get things right first time, although you can have more than one deed of variation if each one relates to a separate gift under the Will.
4 No payment or other consideration must pass between beneficiaries to induce them to enter into the deed of variation (except that a variation is permitted which consists of an exchange of inheritances and a cash adjustment).

Clearly you will need to consult a solicitor or accountant concerning any such deed of variation and the election that needs to be submitted to the Capital Taxes Office of the Inland Revenue.

7 Treatment of insurance policies and sums received from pension schemes

As we explained in Chapter 2, inheritance tax is charged on almost all types of property owned by a person at the date of his death. The amounts paid out by insurance companies and the trustees of pension schemes may well have to be included in the schedule of your assets at death and quite large sums are frequently involved. However, this is an aspect where *careful planning* during your lifetime can bring about *significant improvements* and the right to such payments can usually be excluded from your estate. Moreover, this can often be achieved literally at the stroke of a pen.

Insurance policies

Insurance policies fall into one of the following categories:

- term assurance
- endowment assurance
- whole life assurance
- single premium policies (often called investment bonds).

Let us look at each in turn.

Term insurance

You may have taken out a policy on your own life to cover your family in the event of your dying before a certain date, say in 20 years' time. Normally, such policies have no surrender value and nothing is paid out if you survive to the end of the period.

Because the policy pays out on your death you are called the '**life assured**'. The contract is between you and the assurance company: you contract to pay the premiums, the assurance company contracts to pay out on death. However, there is no reason why the benefits of the policy should be payable to your estate.

The policy could be '**written in trust**' for the absolute benefit of your children etc. This would mean that amounts paid out on your death would belong to them. If the policy were to be written in this way from the outset, the only transfers of value which would take place would be the payment of the premiums. These transfers would normally constitute exempt gifts under the normal expenditure out of income rule (see Chapter 3) and are generally negligible when compared with the amount eventually paid out on the policy.

Most insurance companies provide a range of standard trust wordings so that policies may be written in trust.

There is even an advantage in writing a policy in trust for your wife. No saving of inheritance tax arises because property left under a Will to a spouse is normally exempt. However, there is a considerable *practical* benefit in that the insurance company can pay the proceeds to your widow without requiring probate since the money is payable to the trust direct rather than to the estate.

It may be that you originally took out such a policy in your own name. It can be transferred to your wife, children or put into trust by your **assigning the policy**. This will not normally give rise to any tax complications as the surrender value of such policies is generally nil (although if you were seriously ill the Revenue could ask questions in the event of your early death).

Endowment assurance

An endowment policy is generally a mixture of life assurance and saving. If a person dies, the insurance company pays out the sum assured. If he survives until the end of the period the insurance company pays out a lump sum instead. Some policies can be **unit-linked** to directly link the value of the policy to various types of assets (equities, property etc).

It is possible to write such policies in trust so that the sums paid out on death do not form part of your estate. Furthermore, this can be done in such a way that the lump sum (**sum assured**) still belongs to you if you survive to collect it.

Be careful if you decide to assign an endowment policy which you have had for several years as the transfer of value will be deemed to be the surrender value or the total of the premiums paid, *whichever is the higher.*

Whole of life policies

A whole of life policy requires premiums to be paid throughout a person's life or until age 80 and the insurance company pays out on death. The policy will acquire a surrender value but this type of policy is normally chosen in order to cover inheritance tax arising on death. As such the policy should normally be written in trust.

Single premium policies

These are also called investment bonds and the life assurance element is not normally very great. They can be assigned but this will generally be treated in the same way as a gift of any other investment as they have 'realistic' values from outset.

Sums received from pension schemes

If you are employed by a firm or company and you are a member of a pension scheme, you are likely to have life assurance through the scheme. The Inland Revenue permits a pension scheme to provide 'death in service' cover of up to four times your total remuneration. Death in service cover means that the lump sum is paid out if you die before you retire. Not all pension schemes provide the maximum but most schemes provide life cover of at least twice the employee's pensionable remuneration.

The lump sum may be payable as of right or, more normally, at the discretion of the trustees. If you want the lump sum to be paid to your widow, and you are sure that she will survive you, there is nothing to choose between the two. In other circumstances, it is much better for the lump sum to be paid at the discretion of the trustees.

The reason for this is that if the lump sum is payable as of right it is an asset of your estate (even though you cannot receive it during your lifetime). As such it attracts inheritance tax in the normal way. If the lump sum is payable at the trustees' discretion it is free from inheritance tax.

Where an employee dies in service his family may receive a refund of his contributions together with interest. The sums involved can be quite substantial, especially where the employee has made additional voluntary contributions. If the refund belongs to the estate it is subject to inheritance tax. Once again the amount does not attract inheritance tax if it is payable at the trustees' discretion.

Most modern pension schemes provide a widow's pension of up to two-thirds of the pension that the employee would have received if he had worked till retirement age. The provision of such a benefit to your widow does not have any inheritance tax consequences.

Death benefits provided out of self-employed pension policies or personal pension plans may also be dealt with in a similar way.

8 Passing on your business

This chapter is relevant if you are in business on your own account (a 'sole trader') or in partnership. It also deals with family companies and agricultural property.

Your business may be anything from a sub-post office or newsagent's shop to an engineering consultancy. You may have no employees (apart from your wife and some Saturday part-timers) or you may be in business in a substantial way with a number of partners and a turnover that runs into millions of pounds. Whichever category you fall into, there will almost certainly be some capital involved – especially if you have been in business for some years.

How does the Inland Revenue assess the value of a private business?

The accountants who deal with the business generally negotiate with the Inland Revenue. Most accountants start by looking at the capital that is tied up in the business: the balance on your capital account. They normally then adjust that figure to reflect items in the balance sheet which have a market value that is different from the figures shown. For example, your business assets may include a property at the amount it cost nearly 30 years ago and there may be an asset which is not mentioned at all – goodwill. There may also be some assets which are worth less: your accountant may have allowed for depreciation on your computer over ten years whereas it is now obsolete after only three years.

Valuation is not a precise science. The value to be attributed to goodwill depends upon the nature of the business, whether the profits fluctuate wildly from year to year and a host of other factors. But at the end of the day some compromise will be reached between the accountants and the Inland Revenue.

The agreed valuation is part of your estate for inheritance tax purposes so the Inland Revenue may take a large slice out of your life's work. Fortunately, there are a number of special reliefs and concessions.

Business property relief

Provided that you can meet the essential requirement that you have had your business for at least two years, or had been a partner for at least that time, a 50% deduction is given against the net value of your business property.

EXAMPLE

David has a business with £450,000. On his death the amount charged to inheritance tax is computed as follows:

Value of business	450,000
less 50% relief	225,000
Amount chargeable	225,000

Tax may then be payable at 40% on the £225,000.

The relief is calculated on the net value after deducting bank loans secured against the business assets.

EXAMPLE

Gail was a partner in a business and her interest in the firm was agreed to be worth £400,000. She had borrowed £250,000 to finance her capital investment in the business. Business property relief would be due on £150,000 and not £400,000.

Assets owned by partners rather than the firm

Sometimes partners personally own assets which are used in the business. Gail might, for example, own the office block used by the firm. This would not be a partnership asset as she owned it personally, and charged the firm rent. Nevertheless, business property relief is due but only at a rate of 30%, rather than the full 50% deduction.

Business property owned by trustees

Trustees are eligible for the 50% relief where they own land which is used by the life tenant for the purposes of his business provided that the life tenant himself qualifies for relief in respect of business assets held by him.

Property subject to contract for sale

If there is a binding contract for sale in being at the time of the death (or other capital transfer) no business relief is due. We go into this in Chapter 14 as it could be a problem for partners depending on the way that the partnership deed is worded.

Not all businesses qualify

Most businesses do qualify. Rather surprisingly there is nothing in the legislation which states that the business must be carried on in the UK. Nor is it necessary that the owner had taken an active part in running the business: some assets which qualify are used in businesses which are carried on entirely through agents (for example membership of Lloyd's Underwriting Syndicates). The only restrictions are that the business must not consist wholly or mainly of dealing in securities, stocks or shares, land or building or holding investments.

Not all assets qualify

Business property relief is only given on assets which at the time of death are either:

- used wholly or mainly for the purposes of the business (it is also normally necessary that they have been so used for the previous two years – the 'two year' rule); or
- are required for the future use of the business.

Payment by instalments

Where property qualifies for business property relief the inheritance tax may be paid by interest-free instalments over a period of up to ten years. The instalments are interest-free in that each instalment attracts interest only if it is not paid on time. The outstanding instalments have to be paid if the business property is sold within the ten year period.

A closer look at the two-year rule

Having described the quite considerable benefits which arise if property qualifies as business property, we must look more closely at the two year rule. It is obvious that there should be some minimum period of ownership to prevent 'death bed' arrangements.

The normal rule is that the property should have been owned for two years but if, for example, the property had been inherited from a spouse the period of ownership by the previous owner can be taken into account. Similarly, there are provisions which are intended to cover the situation where a business was sold and the proceeds used to acquire a new business or property. Business property relief will normally be due where the person had carried on qualifying businesses for a total of two years out of the last five years. However, professional advice should be taken as the detailed rules can operate in unexpected and capricious ways.

Treatment of gifts

Business property relief is available on a PET that becomes chargeable only if the necessary conditions are satisfied both at the time of the gift and at the time of death. In practice this means that, if the donor dies within seven years of making a gift of the business, the recipient must have retained his interest in the business or if he has sold out he must have re-invested in a replacement business within 12 months.

EXAMPLE

Clifford gives his son his garage business in 1988 when it is worth £200,000. If Clifford had made a chargeable transfer the 50% relief would have been due. The son does not continue to run the business and sells the assets. If Clifford dies in 1994 he will be deemed to have made a transfer of £200,000 and no business property relief will be done. This could result in additional tax of £40,000 being payable.

Dealing with the family company

Family companies come in all shapes and sizes. J Sainsbury is in one sense a family company even though it has thousands of outside shareholders. However, most of the reliefs are intended for shareholders in *private* companies.

Valuation of shares

The valuation of unquoted shares in private companies is a very difficult part of an accountant's or solicitor's work. There is not usually any established market in the company's shares, indeed the company's articles may well prohibit shares being offered to outsiders. They have to negotiate an estimated market value with a specialist arm of the Capital Taxes Office, the so-called Share Valuation Division.

The underlying assets of the company are largely irrelevant if you have only a relatively small minority shareholding, they may be a more important consideration if you have control. Therefore, a quite different valuation might be placed upon shares which form, say, a 7% shareholding and shares which enable a 51% shareholder to retain control. In the former case the valuers will be looking at factors such as the level of dividends paid in the past and the likelihood of such dividends being paid in the future. At the other extreme, a 51% shareholder would place great value on a 7/51sts part of his shareholding as a disposal of such shares will cause him to lose voting control over the company.

Capital transfer is reduction in donor's estate

Remember that the measure of a capital transfer is the reduction in the donor's estate. We haven't emphasised this aspect previously because much of what we described concerned transfer of land and property, quoted shares and cash. There is not usually a great deal of difference between the value of what the donee receives and the loss in value of the donor's estate which takes place as a result of the transfer. The difference does become quite marked, however, when one looks at gifts of shares in private companies.

EXAMPLE

Harold owns 51 out of the 100 shares in Harold & Son Ltd, a private building company. Valued as part of a controlling shareholding, Harold's shares are worth £1,000 each. Valued as part of a small holding of less than 10%, the shares are worth only £100 each. Valued as part of a large minority shareholding they are worth £700 each. If Harold gives his son and son-in-law one share each he will be making a PET of £16,700:

Value of 51% shareholding at £1,000 per share	51,000
Value of 49% shareholding at £700 per share	34,300
	£16,700

The son and son-in-law, of course, receive shares worth only £100 each.

Related property

There is a special rule where husband and wife own shares in private companies and other similar property or where they are life tenants of trusts which do so. The legislation provides that their holdings shall be aggregated and valued accordingly. This is easiest to illustrate with an example.

EXAMPLE

Suppose that Sydney has 49 shares and his wife has 30 shares. Sydney and his wife have a combined shareholding of 79% (49 + 30) and, when Sydney dies, his shares would be valued as part of a 79% shareholding, ie a much higher value than a 49% shareholding.

In fact, the related property rules go slightly wider than this. If you or your wife have created a charitable trust then shares in the family company held by the trustees in the last five years may need to be taken into account. The effect once again is to treat your shareholding as part of a larger shareholding for valuation purposes.

Sale of related property after death

If the executors or the people who have inherited the related property dispose of it within three years of death and the sale is to an unconnected person, the related property rules may be set aside. The shares etc are then valued at death without taking related property into account.

Business relief

Just as business relief is available to proprietors of unincorporated businesses, it is also available to shareholders in family trading companies who have owned their shares for at least two years. There are, in fact, two rates of relief as shown in Table 6.

Table 6: Rates of business relief

	Rate (%)
Transfer of shares in a trading company (whether quoted or unquoted) where the transferor had voting control before the transfer.	50
Transfer of a property used by a trading company where the transferor had control before the transfer.	30
Transfer of shares in an *unquoted* trading company which gave the transferor control of 25% or more of the voting rights before the transfer.	50
Transfer of other shares in unquoted companies.	30

Companies are treated as quoted if their shares are dealt in on the Stock Exchange or the unlisted securities market (the USM).

Relief is not normally available where the business carried on by the company consists wholly or mainly of dealing in securities, stocks or shares, land or buildings or in making investments. Subject to those limitations, virtually any type of business qualifies.

Relief may be restricted where a company which carries on a qualifying trade also owns investments or other excepted assets. The legislation defines excepted assets as assets which are neither:

- used wholly or mainly for the purposes of the business (it is also normally necessary to have been so used for the previous two years) nor
- required for the future use of the business.

Where a company has subsidiary companies it is necessary to look at the group situation. In other words, shares in subsidiaries may have to be treated as excepted assets if the subsidiaries are investment companies (but not otherwise).

Control   It is necessary that the shares should give voting control. Thus a 50% shareholder who was also the chairman of the company and who, therefore, had the casting vote would not be regarded as a controlling shareholder. This is because the casting vote belonged to him by virtue of his position as the chairman of the company and did not arise through his shares.

Furthermore, it is only the shares which carry the voting rights which attract the 50% relief. If a controlling shareholder had voting and non-voting shares the 50% relief would be due only in respect of the voting shares, the other shares could qualify only for the 30% relief.

Related property   Where shares are valued as related property, the combined shareholding is also taken into account for business relief in seeing whether a person had 25% or 50% of a company.

This is only fair for if when valuing the shares the Inland Revenue aggregate share rights held by husband and wife (and sometimes rights held by a family charitable trust) it is only fair and proper that business relief be calculated on the same basis. Thus shares held by a 20% shareholder in an unquoted company would attract the 50% relief if his wife had a 5% shareholding.

Shares held by trustees   These may be counted for the purposes of the 25% and control tests if the person is the life tenant of the trust.

EXAMPLE

Sidney owes 22% of the shares in Melbourne Ltd. A family trust of which he is the life tenant owns 30%. Sidney will be treated as a controlling shareholder and eligible for the 50% relief.

The trustees are also entitled to claim 50% business relief on Sidney's death.

Ownership   Relief is normally dependent upon the person having held his or her shares for at least two years. On the other hand, the shares need not have given him control or 25% of the voting rights throughout that period. Thus, a person who had held 20 of the 100 shares in issue for two years could qualify in respect of those shares if shortly before he died he acquired another five shares to bring his holding up to 25%.

Where a person had inherited his or her shares from his spouse, the executors can claim that the period of ownership by the original owner should count towards the two year minimum.

Payment by instalments   Inheritance tax on shares which qualify for business relief may be paid by interest-free instalments over a period of up to ten years. Once again, the instalments are interest free in that each instalment attracts interest only if it is not paid on time. The outstanding instalments have to be paid if the shares are sold within the ten-year period.

Reliefs not available if shares are being sold

None of the above reliefs are available if the shares are in the course of being sold or are subject to a binding contract for sale.

Treatment of Gifts

Business relief is only available on a PET that becomes chargeable if the necessary conditions (on pages 66–68) are satisfied both at the time of the gift and at the time of death. This is best illustrated by the following three examples:

EXAMPLE 1

Horace effectively owns all the shares in the family company. He gives his son a 20% shareholding. Three years later the company is sold and the son receives cash for his shares. A year later Horace dies. Business relief will not normally be available as the necessary conditions are not satisfied at the time of death.

If the son has re-invested the proceeds in another private company the relief might not be forfeited.

EXAMPLE 2

As above except that Horace retains his shares. However, by the time that Horace dies the shares are quoted and, therefore, no relief is due.

EXAMPLE 3

Again as above, but this time the shares are retained and are still unquoted at the time of Horace's death. The shares attract the 50% relief to which Horace would have been entitled.

Other problem areas for family companies

We mentioned back in Chapter 3 that certain transactions such as waivers of remuneration and dividends were not normally regarded as constituting transfers of value. The situation in which they most frequently occur in practice is private companies and, therefore, we are going to cover these transactions in this chapter.

Waiver of remuneration

There is an exemption where remuneration is waived. The terms of the exemption are based upon the income tax treatment. In practice the Inland Revenue accepts that

remuneration is not subject to income tax under Schedule E
if it is waived provided:

- the Schedule E assessment has not become final and
  conclusive, and
- the remuneration is formally waived (usually by deed) or,
  if already paid it is repaid to the employer, and
- the employer's assessible profits are adjusted accordingly.

Waiver of dividends

Once again, the legislation reflects the income tax position
and the general law regarding waivers of dividends. A waiver
will be effective for income tax only if it is made before the
person has become entitled to the dividend. Furthermore,
under the general law a waiver cannot be made more than
12 months before the right to the dividend has accrued (it
is not legally possible to waive dividends on a 'standing
order' basis).

The position is slightly different for interim and final
dividends as this governs the date at which the right to a
dividend accrues and, in consequence, the date by which a
deed of waiver must be executed.

Interim dividends   The case law is that a shareholder has no
enforceable right to payment prior to the date on which a
board resolution has declared that a dividend shall be payable.

Final dividends   It is possible that a company might declare
a final dividend without stipulating any date for payment.
In such circumstances the declaration of the dividend creates
an immediate debt and it is, therefore, too late to execute a
waiver. In cases where a final dividend is declared as being
payable at a later date a shareholder may waive his
entitlement provided that he does so before the due date for
payment arrives.

Since an interim dividend may be declared by the directors as payable immediately, whereas a final dividend requires shareholders' approval, it is often thought wise to execute a deed of waiver before the directors meet to consider an interim dividend. In contrast, the waiver of any final dividend may be left until after the directors have met provided that the waiver is made before the company's annual general meeting.

Passing down the family farm and woodlands

The legislation contains special reliefs for agricultural property which reflect the fact that such property is often difficult to sell. Successive Governments have sought to encourage the farming industry and have recognised that many families do not have a great deal of private capital and would have to sell their farm to meet inheritance tax liabilities. The reliefs take the form of a deduction similar to business property relief (but subject to a completely different set of rules) and the right to pay inheritance tax by instalments over a period of ten years.

Agricultural property relief for working farmers

A 50% relief is given by reducing the value of the farmland charged to inheritance tax.

EXAMPLE

When Gerald dies he owns farmland worth £250,000. The 50% agricultural relief is due against the farmland so that the chargeable transfer on Gerald's death is

Farmland	250,000
less agricultural relief	125,000
	£125,000

Agricultural relief is not due on the net assets of the farming business, although they would normally qualify for business relief at the same rate.

This relief is only due on the agricultural value of farmland in the UK, Channel Islands or Isle of Man. The land must actually have been occupied either:

- by the owner
- by a firm in which he is a partner
- by a company of which he is the controlling shareholder for the two years preceding death (or date of gift).

There are similar rules to those governing business property relief to cover the situation where a farmer sells one farm and buys another. The replacement farm normally qualifies provided that the owner has occupied the two farms for a total of at least two years in the last five years. There are certain provisions so that relief is not denied where a person dies within two years of having inherited the farmland from his or her spouse.

Relief for certain let land

Relief is also available on let land provided that the owner may regain vacant possession within 12 months. However, in this case the owner must normally have owned the land for at least seven years (subject to the provisions for replacement land and inheritances).

Relief for tenanted farmland

A 30% deduction is available for farmland which is let and where the owner cannot obtain vacant possession within 12 months. This will generally be the case where the land is let under an agricultural tenancy. Once again, the land must normally have been owned for seven years.

Relief limited to agricultural value

Relief is restricted to the agricultural value of the land and is not available in respect of its development value. The additional value might, in certain circumstances qualify for business property relief.

EXAMPLE

When Charles died he owned farmland worth £1 million. He let it on 364 day licenses and did not farm it himself. The agricultural value is £600,000, the remaining £400,000 is development value.

The agricultural relief would be £300,000 (50% of £600,000). In this particular example there would not be business relief as Charles does not carry on a farming business himself.

If he *had* farmed it himself, there would have been additional business property relief on the £400,000.

Relief only on the net value

Where a loan is secured against agricultural property, the relief is calculated on the net value after taking the loan into account.

EXAMPLE

Mark has secured a loan of £400,000 against farmland worth £700,000. The agricultural relief is due only on the net value of £300,000.

Payment of inheritance tax by instalments

Inheritance tax may be paid by instalments over ten years if either the 50% or the 30% relief is due. These instalments attract interest only if they are not paid by the due date.

Reliefs not available if land subject to contract for sale

None of the above reliefs are available if the land is in the course of being sold or is subject to a binding contract for sale.

Treatment of gifts

Agricultural relief is only available on a PET that becomes chargeable if the necessary conditions are satisfied both at the time of the gift and at the time of death. These conditions are the same as those that apply to business property relief (see pages 60–63).

Grant of an agricultural tenancy

The grant of such a tenancy will usually mean that the market value of the land has gone down, even though the rent which will be charged is a market rent. The legislation expressly covers this and states that granting a lease does not constitute a transfer of value unless the rent payable is less than the market rent.

Woodlands

The treatment of standing timber in the UK is uniquely beneficial as successive Governments since 1918 have maintained various concessions. These concessions reflect the fact that growing timber is a very long-term investment which may not be realised for several generations.

The main benefits are:

1   Business relief is available after two years of ownership.
2   The charge can be postponed until the timber is eventually sold provided that it has been owned for five years.
3   If the charge on standing timber is postponed and the new

owner dies before it is sold, the potential charge is eliminated.

Let us look more closely at the last two of these conditions:

Five-year ownership requirement

The person who has died must have been the owner of the land for five years or he must have acquired it by way of an inheritance or gift. A person who is a life tenant of a trust which owns the land is treated as qualifying.

Effect of an election for postponement

A formal election needs to be submitted within two years of the person's death. The election has the consequence that inheritance tax is not charged on the standing timber (the land itself is still chargeable). When the timber is sold (or otherwise disposed of) the net disposal proceeds or market value must be brought into charge. The rate of tax is governed by the rate which applied on the rest of the person's estate. Business relief is available then if it would have been due had deferment not been claimed.

The net disposal proceeds are the proceeds of the sale of the timber less the costs of re-planting unless they are allowed for income tax purposes (they will not normally be allowable).

The result of electing for deferment is that inheritance tax may be payable on a higher figure but only after a considerable delay.

EXAMPLE

David leaves woodlands worth £100,000 to his son. David's other assets take his estate well over the £110,000 threshold. Business relief is due and, therefore, the inheritance tax that would normally be payable is £20,000. If the son elects for deferment he pays nothing on account of the woodlands (except for the land value). If the son sells the timber for £280,000 30 years later, tax will be payable of £56,000. If he dies before the timber is disposed of, the charge on David's death is eliminated.

9 What can be done? The scope for taking action

You don't have to give away your capital in order to reduce inheritance tax

Outright gifts are a very effective way of avoiding inheritance tax. However, they are not the only possibility. If after reading what follows you do not feel comfortable with making large gifts, don't despair – there is still quite a lot that can be achieved.

The rest of this chapter is addressed mainly at married people with children. You should still read it even if your circumstances are different since many of the general principles will still apply to you. Chapter 16 takes a closer look at the options open to a widowed or divorced person who no longer has a partner. In that chapter, we will also look at the considerations which are relevant to an unmarried person and also to someone who has remarried later in life.

Work out what you can afford to give away

Inheritance tax planning is easier if you are very rich. Someone worth, say, £10 million and aged 65 could reasonably give £9 million to the next generation or put it in trust for them. The remaining £1 million should be sufficient for his needs and provided he lives seven years, he will have avoided inheritance tax of over £3.5 million. Even if he is more cautious, he can probably face giving away £5 million, potentially saving £2 million.

Very few of us are in that happy position. We can't afford to give away half of our capital because we need most of it to live on and so there is less scope for manoeuvre.

There is probably some action along these lines that you could take but you must be careful not to go too far.

Your first priority must be to ensure that you and your spouse will continue to have sufficient income to meet your needs. Nobody should expect you to become a pauper merely in order to save death duties which may not be payable for ten or twenty years. If your heirs do expect you to make substantial sacrifices they almost certainly don't deserve it. You also need to ensure that your widow will have sufficient income to be financially independent after your death.

It's worth stopping at this point. Statistics show that women tend to live longer. If you and your wife are aged 60 and are in good health there is a very good possibility that at least one of you will reach age 75. In fact, the likelihood is that one will live to 80 or beyond. When you consider your income requirements you should look at the figures in this light. Even if the present low rates of inflation remain, they will have a cumulative effect. 5% compound inflation will mean that net income of £10,000 will have a purchasing power equivalent to only £6,250 in ten years time.

Some of your income may be index-linked. Most good company superannuation schemes regularly increase pensions. Similarly, companies tend to increase dividends each year. In times of low inflation these increases tend to keep pace, but in times of rampant inflation they are better than no increases but are not sufficient. At least this is better than the position on fixed-interest investments – the interest paid on bank and building society deposits and conventional gilts does not rise with inflation. The only investments which are guaranteed to increase with inflation are index-linked gilts and nobody should have all his money in such an investment because of the low level of income they produce.

It is very difficult to predict the level of inflation very far into the future. At present the likely prospect is for an average rate of 4–5% per annum between now and the end of the century. However, no-one in 1965 anticipated the very high level of inflation that we experienced in the following ten years and who can definitely say that inflation will not amount to, say, 10% per annum over the next decade?

Be realistic

This is not meant to be alarmist, rather to be realistic. You would be well advised to look at the income you presently enjoy and assume that you will need an income which is much higher in the future. If you are aged 60 and looking ten years ahead, you should anticipate an income at that point in time which will be 160% more than your current income (ten years at 10%. Inevitably, inflation will continue from then until you die, so you should plan on the basis that you will live beyond this and that inflation will continue for the next 20 or so years.

Table 4 shows a rough calculation of what capital may be required in ten years' time.

Table 4:

Present income, say	10,000
Deduct amounts which increase with inflation, say	7,500
Balance	£2,500

Capital currently deployed so as to produce that income, say £30,000.

Capital required in ten years' time to produce an equivalent level of real income: £30,000 × 260% = £78,000

If most of your capital is invested in shares, unit trusts, insurance bonds etc, the income return is less. You currently need, say £50,000 capital to produce net income of £2,500. There is probably less need to double up in such cases – by accepting a lower income now you can reasonably hope that it will keep pace with inflation. Either way, a couple like this probably need to set aside capital of between £50–70,000. They will need less if they are older or are prepared to contemplate living off capital, and more if their pensions do not increase at all (this will often be the situation if you have been self-employed and have had to fund your own pension single-handed).

On this basis, you should not do any inheritance tax planning which reduces your capital below this safety margin. Of course, there are other variables. For example if you die, your widow may not need as much income. On the other hand, medical and nursing bills may mean that you will have to dip into capital in your 80s.

All this sounds excessively conservative and theoretical but it is often borne out by our own experience. We all know people who were comfortably off when they first retired, but who now have to watch their spending more carefully. Ten years ago £30,000 was a large amount of capital so far as most people were concerned, but now it is clearly insufficient to produce a comfortable level of retirement income.

Don't give up

Even if you decide you can't erode your safety margin, there is a great deal that can still be achieved.

Basic strategy

The burden of inheritance tax can be substantially alleviated by a combination of the following:

1 Straightforward methods, for example:
   (a) Equalisation of estates
   (b) Drawing up an appropriate Will
   (c) Making use of annual exemptions.
2 Use of life assurance, ie funding for the potential liability via insurance.
3 The art of gifting:
   (a) Putting any property you inherit into trust (insofar as you can afford to do this)
   (b) Gifts of excluded property
   (c) Gifts of appreciating assets
   (d) Interest-free loans.
4 Creating trusts, especially discretionary trusts, under which your spouse can benefit if necessary.
5 Giving away the family home, thus saving tax. This is often as a last resort.
6 Passing over the family business.

We will look at the ways in which each of these methods can be used in the next few chapters but before then we will look at the straightforward ways of tackling the problem.

Equalisation of estates

As a general principle, it is desirable that you and your spouse should have estates of similar size. You don't know which of you will die first and it would be regrettable if each of you did not make full use of your £110,000 nil rate band. Consider the following example:

EXAMPLE

Ron and Nancy are now elderly. Ron has property worth £250,000. Nancy has nothing in her own name. Nancy dies first. Three months later Ron dies and inheritance tax of £56,000 (£250,000–£110,000 × 40%) is payable. If the property had been divided equally between them, their heirs could have entered into a deed of variation (see Chapter 6) and reduced the inheritance tax payable to £12,000.

This would be achieved by Nancy's property passing to the heirs on her death so that the tax payable on each death would be:

Property passing other than to spouse	125,000
less nil rate band	110,000
	£15,000
Inheritance tax thereon at 40%	£6,000

A similar liability will arise on Ron's death.

Remember that any unused portion of the nil rate band is wasted – there is no provision for transferring the balance to the spouse that survives.

In the past, equalisation of estates was even more important, and it may be so again in the future. Because there was more than one rate of inheritance tax, with the rate going up from 30% to 60% there was considerable benefit in having estates which were equal in value.

EXAMPLE

Suppose Denis and Margaret had died just before the 1988 Budget. The rates of inheritance tax were then as follows:

Value of estate (£)	Rate (%)
First £90,000	Nil
£90–140,000	30
£140–220,000	40
£220–330,000	50
over £330,000	60

An estate worth £350,000 would have attracted tax of £114,000 whereas the tax on £175,000 was only £29,000. Twice £29,000 is only £58,000 – a 'saving' of £56,000.

The rules of this game are apt to change every few years. It may well be prudent to equalise your estates in case the legislation has changed back by the time you die. Certainly, it is very unusual to have one flat rate of death duties as is the case at the present time and this situation cannot be guaranteed to continue for the next 20 years.

Making tax-efficient Wills

This is another area where quite a simple change can save substantial amounts of tax. Let us consider an example.

EXAMPLE

Suppose Ted owns all their property which is worth £200,000. He will have drawn his Will so that everything passes to Eleanor. This means that his £110,000 nil rate band is wasted. When Eleanor eventually dies the £200,000 will form part of her estate and inheritance tax of £36,000 will be payable. If we could persuade him to utilise this there would probably be no inheritance tax payable on either death and a tax saving of £36,000 would be achieved.

Ted may well argue that he has no choice. Of the £200,000 perhaps £120,000 refers to their house and Eleanor needs all the income from the remaining capital of £80,000. However, there is a way of achieving the inheritance tax saving without depriving Eleanor of the income.

Ted might draw his Will so that capital of, say, £60,000 passes into a discretionary Will trust. This uses up part of his nil rate band, as the capital does not pass to Eleanor. On the other hand, there is no reason why she should not be a trustee and, therefore, have a large element of control over the trust fund. More importantly, she can be a beneficiary and in practice might receive almost all the income, although technically this would be paid to her at the trustees' discretion.

The trust fund would not be subject to a charge on her death. When she dies there will probably be a charge as follows:

EXAMPLE

Capital left to her	20,000
House	120,000
	140,000
less nil rate band	110,000
	30,000
Inheritance tax thereon	£12,000

Some readers may ask why Ted should not draw his Will so that all £80,000 of his free money passes into the discretionary Will trust. The short answer is that this may make sense in terms of tax planning but does not cater for the practical realities. A widow needs some money and it is probably right for Eleanor to have complete control over £10–20,000 even though it may cost up to £8,000 in extra inheritance tax. There is a price that should be paid for peace of mind and the £8,000 or so may not be payable for many years if she is much younger or fitter than Ted.

Making use of the annual exemptions

For all the reasons that we have explained, many older people are understandably reluctant to give away a large portion of their capital. On the other hand, there is much less risk attached to giving away surplus income. Some people even look at capital gains in this light – they don't mind making gifts provided that their original capital remains intact.

You may want to mark a special occasion such as your son's wedding by giving him part of the deposit on his new home. When a grandchild is born you may give his parents £250 to invest for the long term. From time to time you may feel able to make use of your annual £3,000 exemption.

Taking action along these lines certainly stops the 'problem' getting worse (if getting 'better off' is a problem!). Gifts covered by the exemptions will be free from inheritance tax immediately. Over ten years you might easily give away, say, £20,000 in this way which saves inheritance tax of £8,000 at present rates. More importantly, it may give you pleasure to share your free income with your children and heirs. You may well think that it is better for them in the long run that from time to time you give them smaller amounts such as £2,000 or £3,000 which they have to husband carefully rather than pass over £20,000 or £40,000 in one go. It also helps you to direct your help where it is most needed.

Sometimes these occasional gifts can be used so as to achieve another tax saving. This is all part of the art of gifting which we go into in the next chapter.

Suppose you have already made capital gains in excess of £5,000 for the current year. You feel that the time is right to sell a particular unit trust but if you do so you may become liable for capital gains tax at either 25% or 40%. A way of making a gift in the most effective way is often to transfer securities and elect for the capital gain to be 'held over'. That means that the gain on a disposal is treated as belonging to the recipient of the gift rather than yourself.

EXAMPLE

Robin decides he is prepared to make a 'one off' present of £6,000 to his daughter Marion. As a quite separate matter he is irked to be told by his accountant that he will be subject to capital gains tax of £1,000 if he sells his ICI shares to produce cash of £6,000.

In fact, Robin can give the ICI shares to Marion and she can then sell them. She will realise a capital gain but this is likely to be covered by her £5,000 annual capital gains tax exemption.

This brings out another important point that it is wrong to look at inheritance tax in isolation – other taxes may also have to be considered.

10 The effective use of insurance

Introduction

Despite all your planning, the end result could be that you
have a potential inheritance tax bill that you cannot avoid.
You need to ensure that you have enough to live on while
you are alive and you need a roof over your head – this can
only be achieved by having a certain amount of capital at your
disposal and this could mean an unavoidable inheritance tax
bill when you die.

Therefore, your heirs will inherit and, if they inherit more
than £110,000, then you have got a tax bill to find.

What is the solution?

There are two choices facing you. You can take no action at
all and leave it to your children to find the money to pay
the tax bill out of their own resources. This could well mean
that they have to sell the possessions that you have left them
in order to raise enough cash to pay the bill.

The other route is to *make plans* now to provide the funds to
pay the bill in the future. Bearing in mind that the bill could
arise at a totally unpredictable time in the future (the date of
your death) the most popular method is one which is *designed*
to provide guaranteed funds at a totally unpredictable time in
the future. This is a life assurance policy.

The solution is almost one that your heirs could take for you. You are giving *them* two choices. Either they can inherit the estate, intact, and then pay tax at 40% on everything over £110,000 (or whatever the rates happen to be at the date of your death) or pay away a small proportion of the potential estate each year into a life policy which will pay the tax bill for them.

The types of policy

In Chapter 7, we covered the main types of insurance policy. They are:

Term assurance   where life cover of a guaranteed amount is paid out if you die during a pre-determined period of time (the term). At the end of the term, that's it. Your life cover ends and you *don't* get any money back. Term assurance is 'pure' insurance and if you don't claim, you get no return.

Endowment assurance   combines life cover with savings. It also has a term but at the end of the term you can anticipate receiving back a lump sum equal to the life cover. These are popular plans for mortgage repayment – if you die during the term, the life cover pays off the mortgage; if you survive, the lump sum pays off the mortgage.

Whole of life   plans provide life cover for as long as you continue paying the premiums. There is a small savings element but the emphasis is on protection.

In general, whole of life assurance is the solution for inheritance tax planning. You also have a choice of structure and this is important because, if you are married, the inheritance tax liability normally occurs when the *second* person dies. Therefore, you should arrange a 'joint life, second death' plan.

The final point is to beware of a Catch 22 Situation. You work out your potential tax bill and take out a policy to cover this. Then, when you die, the proceeds of the policy are added to your estate – which means a *bigger* tax bill. The solution is a simple trust which will be sorted out – usually at no charge – by the life company. Your children will be the beneficiaries and so the proceeds of the policy go to them, and they now have the funds to pay the taxman.

That, of course, means that the policy is theirs, but you are paying the premiums. The premiums are therefore **gifts**, but they will usually be covered by one of the exemptions.

This type of arrangement, **a joint life, second death, whole of life policy written in trust,** is one of the most common forms of life assurance policy, specifically designed to provide for a future inheritance tax bill.

The way in which it can work

The basic ideas of using life assurance are often quite straightforward but the way that they can be combined can be very impressive in reducing the problems posed by inheritance tax to manageable propositions. The inherent advantages of insurance policies as a tool in dealing with inheritance tax are:

- the element of certainty that an insurance policy provides
- the flexibility of modern insurance policies.

Certainty and peace of mind

We have already suggested that a very effective way of making use of the exemption for normal expenditure and the annual £3,000 exemption is to fund a whole of life policy. A considerable level of cover may be obtained for an annual contribution of £3,000. For a husband and wife both aged 60 the standard cover could be about £180,000 and even if you are both 70 the cover might still amount to about £90,000.

Obviously the cover might be less if you and/or your spouse are not in excellent health, but the level of cover may still represent very good value even after the terms of the policy had been adjusted to reflect medical problems.

Now it has to be said that you could fund the liability directly. If you religiously set aside £3,000 per annum and gave it to your heirs, and if you ensured that they invested it and reinvested the income, then you could accumulate a sizeable sum in their hands which could be used to cover the inheritance tax which will fall due on your death. Suppose that the average life expectancy for a person of your age is 18 years. Also assume (and it is a big assumption) that your relatives will be able to manage the money and achieve a good rate of return after tax, in bad as well as good periods for the stock market. Suppose they achieve an average 7% return, at the end of 18 years they will have accumulated £109,000. That would seem to suggest that one could make do without using an insurance company but for most people that would constitute a big mistake.

The whole point is that an average life expectancy is just that – an average. Some people will live longer, some will not live so long. Suppose you did embark upon the above DIY plan but you died after only ten years. Your family would probably have accumulated only about £45,400 by then and this would fall well short of the amount required. One cannot emphasise too strongly the benefits of the certainty and peace of mind that insurance provides, to say nothing of the fact that your money goes into funds which are *managed by professionals*.

Flexible nature of modern insurance policies

Many companies now offer whole of life plans where the level of cover can be varied from time to time. Of course, the greatest benefit arises if you start these plans in middle age (or even before).

EXAMPLE

Barry and Maureen are aged 50 and 45 years respectively. Now that their children are off their hands they have surplus income of £3,000 per annum and they decide to put £1,000 of this into a flexible whole of life plan written in trust for their children (this is done so that it does not form part of their estate). The amount of the cover starts off at £158,000 and can be increased each year. The remaining £2,000 is put into a maximum investment plan (also written in trust for their children).

After ten years the cover on the whole of life plan has increased to around £300,000 and the premiums to £2340. They are now finding it more difficult to pay the premiums out of their income.

Assuming a 7% annual growth in the value of units, the maximum investment plan will have a cash-in value after ten years of around £30,000. The maximum investment plan can then be cashed-in with no tax liability and the proceeds can be used to fund the premiums on the whole of life policy. When Barry and Maureen die the position might be as follows:

Capital from maximum investment plan	£30,000
Proceeds from whole of life policy	£300,000
Available to cover inheritance tax	£330,000

Funding the tax that will eventually be payable

Some people have sufficient disposable income to enable them to take out insurance which completely covers their

inheritance tax liability. This is often not that expensive if
you start taking out policies before you get too old, say in
your 50's or early 60's. On the other hand a lot of people
consciously decide that they will not try to cover all the tax
payable on their deaths but do decide to take out some
insurance. It's a fine thing for a family if you can afford to
go all the way but this attitude is perfectly understandable.
It's a question of priorities. However, the point to recognise
is that some insurance is generally thought to be most
desirable, if not essential.

How do you work out the level of cover that is needed? This
must vary according to your circumstances, but it may be
helpful if we tell you how many people approach this matter.
Some people say that what really concerns them is that their
children will have to sell the family home or other assets
which have been in the family for many years. Similarly,
where a person has spent his life building up a business or
family company he naturally hates the thought of his life's
work being sold because money for death duties cannot be
found in any other way. In other words, those people regard
insurance as a way of ensuring that their heirs can afford to
retain certain property.

Some people look at matters slightly differently. They are
anxious to avoid a situation where executors have to sell
assets in a poor market to meet death duties. They say their
children will be much better off than they were at that stage
in their own lives, even after the taxman has taken his slice.
They have no particular inclination to stint themselves just
in order to pass over even more but they do feel they want
to make a contribution to give their family a financial
'breathing space'. After all, it was particularly unfortunate for
heirs in 1973 or 1974 if the executors had been forced to sell
stocks and shares at the very bottom of the market. It would
be equally regrettable if a house had to be sold at any price
during a difficult period, whereas by hanging on for (say) two
years the family could get an amount which fully reflected
its value.

Which type of policy?

Whichever category you fall into, you should get some quotes. You know what you can afford to pay without suffering hardship, ask for details of the cover that this will provide on a whole life basis.

Think about the effects of the way that you have drawn your will. If most of your property will pass to your spouse and the inheritance tax will actually be payable on his or her death, the joint life last survivor insurance may be appropriate. This is a policy where the insurance company pays out on the death of the survivor, ie when both you *and* your wife or husband have died. The premiums are bound to be cheaper and the money will arrive when it is really needed, and not before.

Insurance companies can be flexible. Their business is providing a range of standard products which meet people's requirements. Some policies may fit your requirements better than others. For example, most quotes will show a premium calculated on the basis that it will be payable until both you and your spouse have died. On the other hand, you may feel it is unfair to saddle your widow with the burden of paying heavy annual premiums. If that is how you look at it you should get quotes for a joint life last survivor policy where the premiums stop on the first death. Similarly, you may anticipate that after, eg, ten years you may find the premiums a strain on your finances. Don't be put off, some unit linked policies are designed with this option in mind.

A fairly simple 'solution' with no complications

For many people, the following approach can be attractive:

1   Take, say 20% of your investment capital.

2   'Dedicate' this for the next ten years or so to cover a large
    amount of your inheritance tax liability.
3   Feel free to deal with the rest of your assets as you please
    – and with a good conscience.

EXAMPLE

Ron and Sylvia are both aged 60 and have investment capital of £200,000.
They set aside £40,000 and use the income from this to fund premiums
of £2,000 per annum on a flexible whole life plan written in trust for their
children. Their other income is sufficient for their needs. The policy pays
out on the death of the survivor. If they were both to die the policy would
pay out about £125,000. After the first death the survivor could discontinue
payment of premiums and cover would then continue at a lower rate. For
example, if Ron died after ten years, and Sylvia discontinued payments
of premiums, cover of about £70,000 could be maintained indefinitely
provided units grow at 7% per annum. Alternatively full cover could be
maintained for a further 12 years approximately.

We are not saying these options would necessarily be the right
thing to do but they do show how flexible insurance policies
can provide high levels of cover in a way that fits in with
changed circumstances. Sylvia might want to discontinue
premiums because her widow's pension was only half of her
husband's pension.

If Ron dies at age 77 (his life expectancy at age 60 is 17 years)
the full cover of £125,000 could be maintained for about 10
years without any further premiums being payable subject to
satisfactory investment performance.

The way the tax laws can help

Life assurance is not solely the domain of the traditional life
assurance policy. There are other forms of investment that
also have important life assurance elements that can be a
useful part of your personal financial planning. Not only
that, the way the tax laws work means that these plans can
also have significant benefits for inheritance tax planning.

Pension plans

Contributions to a personal pension plan are free of tax at the highest rates of tax you pay. Not only that, the contributions are invested in a fund which pays no UK taxes at all, giving it greater potential for growth than, say, a life assurance fund which is taxed.

On death, the pension plan will usually pay out either the value of the fund or the total of all gross contributions paid into the fund. This sum will, in most cases, be paid out to your estate totally free of any liability to inheritance tax.

This provides a way for directors of family companies to pass money to their estate if they should ever find themselves in a position where life assurance is expensive. This is most likely to occur with older people who have neglected to make their life assurance arrangements in time or, more unfortunately, people who are in poor health and where the life company would certainly charge additional premiums for any given level of life cover. Through their pension plan, they are able to make some provision for their families in a way which is tax efficient from the point of view of inheritance tax.

EXAMPLE

Peter is aged 59 and earning £35,000. His company ought really to have set up a pension scheme long before but it had not done so. The company could normally pay a contribution of £140,000 or so without any problem in obtaining Revenue approval. Tax relief would in due course normally reduce the net cost to between £91,000 and £105,000. In addition, Peter could pay £5,250 (15% of £35,000) out of his pre-tax income. On death, the insurance company could pay out the £145,250 completely tax free. In principle, all this could be done within a week or so of death.

Nobody likes to consider such a possibility. The fact remains that the law on pension schemes can provide a means of mitigating the financial consequences of bereavement. It probably won't be sufficient but it can be a major step in the right direction, leaving the family to cope with the human aspects of the situation.

Using bonds to provide your spouse with tax deductible income

Single premium bonds are lump sum investments issued by life assurance companies. They are, in effect, lump sum life policies but where there is significantly greater emphasis placed on investment. Typically, the maximum amount of life cover built into the investment is 150% of the value of the investment falling to 1% for older lives.

Nevertheless, they *are* life policies and so can be taken out on a joint life basis and can also be written in trust. This gives them some useful feature when it comes to planning for inheritance tax.

EXAMPLE

Suppose Clive and Marion each have £110,000 to invest. They are in their late 60's. Their requirements are income during their joint lives, a degree of security for the survivor and maximising the net estate passing to their children and grandchildren.

They should proceed as follows:

1   Clive takes out a £110,000 single premium bond in his own name, but on the joint lives of himself and his wife. He is the sole owner of the policy. Marion similarly takes out a bond on the joint lives of the couple, but owned solely by her.
2   The bonds are not put in trust or gifted in any other way.
3   The couple take annual withdrawals in order to give them an income whilst they are both alive. (Up to 5% of the original investment can be withdrawn each year without any liability to income tax at the time.)

4 Clive dies. Neither bond becomes a death claim, because only one of the two lives assured has died. The bond owned by Marion continues to be held by her, and she is free to continue drawing cash from the bond as and when necessary.

5 The bond formerly owned by Clive is left by him in his Will, to be held under the terms of a trust for the benefit of their children or grandchildren. Regardless of which type of trust is used, the trustees should have the power:
   (a) to advance capital to Marion
   (b) to pay income to her.
   (c) to lend money to her.

6 The trustees meet regularly – perhaps once a year or every six months to decide how best to meet the needs of all the beneficiaries. If they think it appropriate, they could lend money to the widow for her to use as the thinks fit, the loans being interest-free and repayable on demand.

This will have the following inheritance tax implications:

1 On the first death the value of the bond to be held in trust will be taxable in the normal way. If it does not exceed the nil rate band and Clive has made no other chargeable transfers in his lifetime (including PET's during the seven years before death) there will be no tax to pay. The bond held in trust will not be taxable on Marion's death. Any growth on the bond held in trust will also be outside of Marion's estate.

2 Any loans granted to Marion will be deductible for inheritance tax purposes. The anti avoidance legislation mentioned in Chapter 20 does not apply since it comes into operation only when the deceased person has taken loans from a person to whom he has made lifetime gifts.

3 The inheritance tax savings will depend upon how long Clive and Marion live and the rate of growth within the bond. Assuming that Clive dies after five years and Marion dies ten years later and taking a 7% pa rate of growth, the position would be:

Tax-free income taken by Clive during his lifetime (5,500 × 5)	£27,500
Tax-free 'income' taken by Marion (5,500 × 15)	£82,500
Loans to Marion	£55,000
Value of bonds on Marion's death (approximately)	£300,000

The inheritance tax payable would depend upon the rates in force at that time. However, it is likely to be fairly modest since Marion's estate is deemed to be as follows:

Value of her bond (approximately)	£150,000
Less loans from Clive's Will trust	£55,000
	£95,000

Get advice on insurance from a specialist

The possibilities for constructive use of insurance are legion and you really need to consult a specialist. He will need to know the value of your capital, your present net income after tax and your income requirements for the future. It may also be helpful if you prepare a schedule of your existing insurance arrangements showing the annual premiums, the sum assured and the date that each policy comes to an end.

Assumptions

In this chapter (and elsewhere) use has been made of various inheritance tax planning devices using life assurance and other investments. In all the examples, an annual growth rate of 7% has been assumed – the lower of the two rates recommended in guidelines issued by Lautro (the other assumed rate of growth allowed by the guidelines is 10½%). It must be remembered that this **is** only an assumption. Growth rates in practice could be lower or higher and the value of investments can fall as well as rise.

11 The art of gifting

In the last two chapters we looked at the things that you should consider before parting with a major portion of your capital and what can still be achieved even if you don't feel able to do so. We started to explain a simple strategy involving equalisation of estates, tax-efficient Wills, use of annual exemptions, and insurance. In this chapter we will look at the art of gifting.

Let's first examine the aspects that should be considered before you make any large gift:

- Can you afford to make this gift?
- Will the recipient use it wisely?
- Can you give it away but still enjoy some benefit?
- Should you defer making the gift?
- Is there a time limit in which you must make up your mind?
- Can it be passed on equally well by your Will?
- Is it better to give money or property?
- Can or should any strings be attached?
- Are there any other taxes to be considered?

Some of the above are personal considerations whereas this book confines itself mainly to financial matters. Other questions have been considered already, particularly in the previous chapter. You should continue to bear them in mind as we consider further suggestions.

Putting any property you inherit into trust

You may be a beneficiary under a relative's Will or you may be a beneficiary under a family trust. Perhaps your father created a Will trust and you recently became entitled to the fund on your mother's death. The question is whether you should merge your inheritance with your own assets or pass it over to your children etc. Tax experts refer to this as 'generation skipping' and it certainly makes sense on paper provided that you feel comfortable about 'handing over what you have never had'.

The way that you should do this is generally through a deed of variation or a disclaimer. You may recall that you have two years to execute such a variation, ie two years from the date of the death which gave rise to your entitlement. Once you have executed the deed and submitted the elections the arrangement is effective. There is an important advantage in doing things this way: you do not have to survive seven years to avoid a 'claw-back'.

There may also be another advantage. As we have seen, it is not normally possible to make a gift and reserve a benefit, but gifts effected through a deed of variation are different. The effect of a deed of variation is that the property which is redirected is treated as if it passed in accordance with the deceased person's Will. The person who effectively relinquishes part or all of his entitlement is not treated as making a transfer of value.

Some tax specialists are of the opinion that it is possible for you to enter into a deed of variation whereby the property you would otherwise have received is put into a discretionary trust under which you are yourself a potential beneficiary. The reservation of benefit rule may not apply because you are not making a transfer of value so far as the inheritance tax legislation is concerned.

The position if you want to disclaim a benefit under a trust is less flexible. You cannot redirect the property since disclaiming simply means that you drop out of the picture. What happens next depends upon the terms of the trust. Very often the effect is that your children stand in your place, but you will need to confirm the position with your solicitor.

It is really best to anticipate this situation and arrange matters before your reversionary interest falls in. This brings us to the next point.

Gifts of excluded property

You may have a reversionary interest under a family trust where you will become entitled to the trust property on the death of the life tenant who receives the trust income for the time being. It is possible to assign the benefit of such an interest but a person who does so is *not* regarded as making a transfer of value. The interest is regarded as 'excluded property', ie an asset which is ignored for inheritance tax purposes.

Suppose your mother is entitled to a life interest under your father's Will. On her death the Will trust provides that the property is divided between you and your sister. You can give the benefit of your future rights to your children or, once again, you can transfer these rights to a discretionary trust (although it would be strongly advisable to get professional advice as transferring your interest to a trust is not necessarily straightforward).

Gifts of appreciating assets

Another obvious strategy, when you think about it, is to give away capital growth investments. This is attractive for two reasons. These type of investments do not normally yield very much income and so you are not giving up much in terms of spendable income. Also, the long-term benefit is greater than if you give away assets which do not grow in value.

You should also bear in mind that by giving away an asset you fix the maximum amount that will be included in your estate at the present fairly low value. The future appreciation escapes inheritance tax even if you do not manage to survive seven years.

EXAMPLE

Audrey has invested in 3% Treasury Stock 1998. It will be redeemed at par in May 1998 but the present price of £100 stock is only £70. If Audrey gives away £20,000 nominal stock the amount which will be chargeable will be £14,000 even though when she dies in six years' time the stock may have a market value of £90 per £100.

Gifts of property or shares have shown even more appreciation over a period of six years. Furthermore, the fact that there is relief if the value goes down means that this is a 'one-way bet' against the Inland Revenue.

Gifts of depreciating assets

Very occasionally there will be exceptions to the general rule. Suppose you wish to help your son pay his children's school fees. You could give him £20,000 to cover the next six or seven years' fees. Alternatively, you could invest £20,000 in a seven-year annuity and assign this asset to him. If you do die in six years' time the market value of the asset may be only £3,000 and it will be this amount which attracts tax as a PET!

Do bear in mind that this is the exception that proves the rule. There are special rules covering gifts of chattels, rights

over land and securities. Take professional advice where
substantial sums are involved.

Interest-free loans

When capital transfer tax, the forerunner of inheritance tax,
was introduced in 1974 the nil rate band was £15,000. Today
it is £110,000. Think of the huge saving in tax which could
have been achieved if a person 'froze' his estate in 1974 and
ensured that *all* growth in value went directly to his family
rather than being added to his estate. This is an extreme
example, you probably wouldn't feel able to go this far but
you might be prepared to commit a part (say £50,000) in
this way, especially if you were able to 'unscramble' the
arrangement at short notice if your circumstances required
it.

One very straightforward way of achieving this is to make an
interest-free loan. Normally, the loan should be repayable
upon demand (see page 24). You could make the loan to
trustees to ensure that you do not lose control. They would
put the money on deposit and earn interest which they would
pay over to the beneficiary of the trust, eg your son or
daughter or grandchild.

Alternatively, you could cut out this administration and
simply lend, eg, your son, the money direct. However, if
large sums are involved do take care to ensure that he will
be in a position to pay you back at short notice if this is
necessary.

Another variation on this theme is to set up a simple trust
with your son or daughter etc as the main beneficiary.
Unfortunately, you must not be a potential beneficiary
yourself. You can then lend the trust, say £20,000.
Technically, the loan will be repayable on demand but you
can assure the trustees that in practice you will use your best

endeavours to give a much longer period of notice. This enables them to invest the £20,000 on a longer-term basis.

Suppose they invest in an insurance bond and the bond grows in value by an average of 7% per annum. In ten years' time the bond will be worth around £38,000. The bit that effectively belongs to you will still be £20,000 (ie your loan). The rest is held for the benefit of your son, daughter etc and is not part of your estate.

The above figures have been chosen advisedly. Whether it is right to make a loan of £20,000 or £50,000 or even £100,000 depends upon your circumstances. But assuming that someone can afford to make an interest-free loan of £50,000 on a short-term basis, he ought not to tie up more than £20,000 or so in what is effectively a longer-term arrangement.

Seven-year trusts

Yet another variation on this theme is to set up a temporary or 'seven-year' trust. This may seem a digression but the connection is that if you create a trust under which your grandchildren are the beneficiaries for the next seven years and the property then comes back to you, the practical implications are much the same as if you made a seven-year interest-free loan.

Advantages of doing this rather than making a loan

The principal advantage is that your grandchildren may be able to make use of their income tax allowance and enjoy the income tax-free. This benefit could amount to a current maximum of £651 (ie 25% of the single person's allowance) per grandchild for *each year* without costing you anything extra.

Previously you could have achieved this by making a seven-year deed of covenant in their favour but the Chancellor has abolished this method of transferring income, at any rate for deeds of covenant made after March 1988. The above suggestion involving a short-term trust is in effect a long winded way of achieving the tax benefits formerly obtained by deeds of covenant in a way that has escaped Mr Lawson's axe. Once again it shows how we should be alert to possible ways of securing other tax benefits when we set out to save inheritance tax.

The trust will also enjoy its own annual capital gains tax exemption. This could be as much as £2,500 and will certainly be at least £500 for 1988/89, depending upon whether you have set up any other trusts during your lifetime. This is another benefit which, although small, should not be ignored.

Minimum requirements 'of seven-year' trusts

The trust must last for at least seven years – your grandchildren etc can have an entitlement to income for a longer period if you so wish, but seven years is the minimum period. (Actually this is an income tax requirement; it just happens that seven years is also an important period of time for inheritance tax.)

The trust deed may provide for the property to revert to you once the seven years are up but it would probably be better if the trust deed excluded you and instead provided that the property would then be held upon discretionary trusts with your wife being one of the class of potential beneficiaries. This is likely to produce a better inheritance position even if you die within seven years of creating the trust, and the trust property will be outside your estate once that period has elapsed.

Other types of trust

This leads us on to the wider subject of the use of trusts in general, and the practical aspects of setting one up. This subject warrants a chapter to itself.

12 Using trusts

In the last chapter we introduced the idea of a specific kind of trust. This brings us to consider the general advantages of making large lifetime transfers by putting money into trust rather than making outright gifts. The main advantages are:

1   Trusts are a very effective way of giving property 'with proper strings attached'. You may want to make sure that the capital you give away is applied for specific purposes or, at any rate, is not frittered away. Once you have made an *outright* gift you have no way of ensuring this.
2   You can retain a large measure of control either by appointing trustees who will pay due regard to your views and wishes, or even by being a trustee yourself.
3   You can make provision for your spouse to benefit in future to cover your position if her financial circumstances change for the worse.
4   There are a few limited circumstances in which you can benefit under your trust without being caught by the gifts with reservation rule.

It has to be recognised that many people are suspicious of the whole idea of trusts. This may be because of an unfortunate experience in their family, ('Uncle Anthony tied up all his money in trust which meant it had to be invested in War Loan and Auntie Dorothy couldn't draw on it when she needed to do so'). Other people are put off by the complexity ('I hate being asked to sign an 18-page document that I don't really understand'). Another minus factor is the cost ('. . . in the end the trustees' annual fees swallowed up nearly a quarter of the annual income').

The truth is that there *is* something in those worries and there are pitfalls of making a trust which is not appropriate to your family's circumstances or making the wrong sort of trust which is inflexible. However, there ought to be good reasons for having 18 pages – many trust deeds (ie the document which regulates the trust) are set out in a single page and if a larger deed is appropriate then a good solicitor will explain why, and sit down with you in order to explain what each section really means. There are good and bad trusts just as there are Wills which are well thought out and Wills which create nearly as many problems as they solve. So do approach the subject with an open mind.

Let's look at the main types of trust.

Interest in possession trusts

A common form of trust is one that takes the following form:

The property shall be held on trust so that Simon shall be entitled to the income. The trust capital shall pass to Simon on his 25th [or 35th or 40th] birthday. If Simon shall die before that date then the capital shall pass in the following way . . .

Of course, the trust deed may not read like that; lawyers have their own technical vocabulary like any other specialists, but that is what it really comes down to. Also, it does not have to be the 25th or 35th or 40th birthday. It could be any age (but it must not be younger than 18).

There may be further provisions, eg the trustees may have the power to pass over the capital to Simon before he reaches the specified age (but not before his eighteenth birthday), if they are satisfied that doing this is in their best interests. The trust deed may also say what should happen if Simon is made bankrupt. If he dies before the capital vests, ie before he becomes entitled to it), the trust deed may say that his children (if there are any) should stand in his shoes. The deed should specify what must be done if Simon dies prematurely and without having children.

Making such a trust helps you to ensure that the capital is not used by Simon for a purpose that you think he may regret in the longer term. The trustees can always pass capital over if they are satisfied that it is needed for a good purpose. They may well consult you for your views. A trust of this nature may well be appropriate if you wish to make provision for a mentally handicapped child who is not capable of managing his financial affairs.

From an inheritance tax point of view, the creation of such a trust is a PET and the capital will not form part of your estate unless you die within the seven-year period.

You should take professional advice from an accountant or solicitor, but unless the trust deed is badly drafted there should be no question of your being subject to income tax on the trustees' income. Even if this were so, the tax would actually be payable by the trust rather than out of your own pocket.

Accumulation and maintenance trusts

You will recall from Chapter 5 that an accumulation and maintenance trust must provide that at least one beneficiary will have an interest in possession not later than attaining the age of 25. In practice, these trusts often provide that the beneficiaries become entitled to income at the age of 18 or 21. The capital need not vest at that time – one could have a qualifying accumulation and maintenance trust where the capital remained in trust until the beneficiary concerned attains the age of 40, or even beyond.

Whilst the grandchildren or other beneficiaries are under 18 etc, the trustees can accumulate the income or distribute it to the child's parents for it to be used for his or her 'education or maintenance'. The income received by the trustees is subject to tax at the basic rate (25%) plus an additional rate of 10% until a child becomes entitled to an interest in possession when the rate of tax goes down to just the basic rate (25%). On the other hand, where income is distributed it generally counts as the child's income and part or all or the 35% tax may often be recovered. Different rules apply if the beneficiaries are your own children rather than grandchildren.

Once again the use of a trust enables you to control the way that the capital is used. A more complicated accumulation and maintenance trust deed will allow the trustees to discriminate between the various beneficiaries and this further element of control may sometimes be desirable.

Creating an accumulation and maintenance trust involves making a PET.

Discretionary trusts

Stripped of legalese a discretionary trust usually provides something like this:

The trustees shall hold the trust fund until the appointed day and shall use the income to make payments to any one of the specified class as they shall in their absolute discretion decide. The trustees may also distribute capital if they so decide. At the appointed day the trust fund shall be distributed as follows . . .

The appointed day may be a date up to 80 years after the trust was created. The specified class may be very narrowly defined, eg 'my wife, daughter and any present or future grandchild', or it may be widely defined, eg 'any lineal descendant of my great-grandfather who shall at the time be either resident or ordinarily resident in the UK'.

The trustees may have power to accumulate income, ie not to pay it out but to reinvest it. They may or may not have power to distribute capital. Some trust deeds provide that the settlor's written consent is required before they can do this during his lifetime.

In the main, it is unlikely that the trust will not have been wound up long before the appointed day arises, but if the fund remains in being then the deed will probably say that it shall be divided equally between the members of the specified class, or something along those lines.

The trust deed will often set out what should happen if there are no members of the specified class still alive on the appointed day. It usually names 'default' or 'long-stop' beneficiaries who will take the fund by default if the family etc has died out. Many people name charities as default beneficiaries.

When is a discretionary trust appropriate?

A trust of this nature requires careful thought. On the one hand it is a very flexible 'vehicle' which can be used to hold family money. The trustees can apply the money to meet changing circumstances and needs. On the other hand, one is passing over considerable powers of discretion to the trustees and one must choose the trustees carefully. Some settlors like to retain the power to appoint fresh trustees in case they do not approve of the decisions taken by the trustees they appointed in the first instance.

An important benefit is that you can name your wife or husband as one of the specified class of beneficiaries. The Inland Revenue have confirmed that this does not of itself constitute the reservation of a benefit.

The fact that this possibility exists may enable you to pass over more capital than you are prepared to give away on an absolutely irrevocable basis. Of course, if the trustees pay money out to your spouse and she or he acts as a 'conduit', and pays it straight over to you, the Revenue may well look at things entirely differently.

One recommended route is to form four or five smaller trusts rather than one big one. The reason for this is that if *any* benefit percolates back to the settlor it can cause the gift with reservation rule to apply. Far better for one £10,000 trust to be 'caught' because you received, say, £1,000 via your wife, and for the four other trusts to remain untainted, than if a single £50,000 trust was invalidated.

Bear in mind that if your spouse is a potential beneficiary the income received by the trustees may attract tax at your top rate. The trustees will, however, have to reimburse you for any extra tax that you are required to pay. Furthermore, this is less of a problem now that the top rate of income tax has been reduced to 40% – the maximum extra tax that could apply is normally 15% (and even this may fall away when the proposed new rules for taxing husband and wife are introduced in 1990). Even this does not apply if your spouse can only benefit after your death, ie as your widow rather than your wife. The trustees then pay tax at 35% and once again this can often be recovered by the beneficiaries if the income is distributed (see 'Accumulation and maintenance trusts', above).

Not all trusts are complicated

Many trust deeds are quite straightforward, especially those used in connection with insurance policies and many deeds consist of only one page.

Costs

It is difficult to give an estimate of the costs of having a firm of solicitors draw up a trust deed as it depends how complex your requirements are and the extent to which 'precedents' have to be adapted to meet your circumstances. However, charges often fall within the range of £300–750.

Insurance companies do not normally make a charge for providing suitable trust documents in connection with insurance policies.

Creating a trust

As always, we must consider the effect of other taxes rather than looking at inheritance tax in isolation. Fortunately, the news is good. There is normally no liability for stamp duty on creating a trust beyond a nominal 50p charge. If you want to transfer securities or other property to a trust you can avoid an immediate liability for capital gains tax provided that the trust is resident in the UK.

EXAMPLE

Harry and Frances have a portfolio of stocks and shares which cost them £50,000 and are now worth £90,000, and they want to set up a trust. If they sold the shares and put the proceeds into trust they would realise chargeable gains of £40,000 (ignoring indexation relief). Instead, they can transfer the securities and elect for the disposal to be treated as giving rise to neither gain or loss for capital gains tax purposes. The trust then takes over their acquisition value of £50,000. As and when securities are sold, the trust becomes liable for capital gains tax.

Putting business property into trust

Trusts are an especially effective way of avoiding inheritance tax on family businesses and private companies. This is covered in more detail in Chapter 14.

13 The matrimonial home

The house or flat where you live is probably your most valuable single asset. It is also an asset which does not produce any income. Many older people wonder whether there is any action that they can take whereby they can make their property exempt from inheritance tax even though they continue to live there.

There are indeed schemes which are intended to achieve this, but be very careful. It is just as important to investigate the personal implications as it is to work out what needs to be done to avoid inheritance tax.

That is not to say that nothing can be done. We are going to examine some possibilities, looking first at the more straight-forward and less risky arrangements.

Holding property as 'tenants in common'

You may own your house etc in your own name, or jointly with your spouse. The normal form of joint ownership is where ownership of the property 'accrues' to the survivor. In other words, if you and your spouse own the house in your joint names your spouse will become the sole owner on your death (and vice versa). With this sort of ownership, your share of the house is not something that you can transfer through your Will, ownership passes automatically. This is called the right of 'survivorship'.

Let's consider the implications of this. Suppose your spouse does not own much property and dies before you. The nil rate band may be wasted. We have previously considered that estates be equalised as far as is convenient. It is often very helpful if a spouse has a separate interest in the matrimonial home which can be left directly to your children so as to make use of the nil rate band. Alternatively, it may be a good idea to give your spouse such an interest so that full advantage can be taken of a deed of variation if this should be appropriate.

It may be that you would like to transfer your half-interest. For example, your estate may consist of stocks and shares worth £80,000 and the family home. You feel that you must leave the £80,000 to your spouse to provide income and you would like to bequeath your interest in your home to your children, thereby utilising *your* nil rate band.

There is a way of opening these various possibilities. Joint ownership of property can fairly easily be converted into the other form of joint ownership where you and your spouse would have rights as 'tenants in common'. Holding property in this way is for all practical intents and purposes the same as joint ownership except that the rights of 'survivorship' do not apply. Each 'tenant in common' may, therefore, transfer ownership of his or her interest in the property.

It is probably a good idea for some people to hold their property in this way. The legal costs involved in converting joint ownership into a tenancy in common are fairly small and no stamp duty is normally payable. Doing this will give you and your family more flexibility in dealing with your property on the death of you and your spouse.

Actually drawing your Will so that your interest passes directly to your children is another matter and one which needs careful consideration. A tenant in common may require the property to be sold and the proceeds divided – do you want your widow/widower to have to face such an eventuality? It may save £44,000 inheritance tax on the nil rate band in the long run, but is it worth it if it causes your spouse real anxiety and heartache? You may think you know your children would not take such action but people do change. In any event, it may not be their doing – suppose you leave your interest in the family home to your son who is then divorced and is obliged to raise capital to comply with a court order?

Another point to bear in mind is that the survivor may not be able to sell the house, move somewhere smaller and realise the capital.

At the end of the day, this is something which you alone can decide. However, we do recommend that you talk through these issues with your spouse and that you take advice from a solicitor.

Gift of an interest to a child etc who lives with you

It may well be that a son or daughter lives with you and you wish to pass over part of the value of your home. Some concern was felt that if a person did this it would be caught by the gift with reservation rules. Fortunately, this point was cleared by a statement in the House of Commons by a Treasury Minister who said on 10 June 1986:

. . . it may be that my Hon Friend's intention concerns the common case where someone gives away an individual share in land, typically a house, which is then occupied by all the joint owners including the donor. For example, elderly parents may make unconditional gifts of undivided shares in their house to their children and the parents and their children occupy the property as their family home, each owner bearing his or her share of the running costs. In those circumstances, the parents' occupation or enjoyment of the part of the house that they have given away is in return for similar enjoyment of the children of the other part of the property. Thus the donors' occupation is for a full consideration.

Accordingly, I assure my Hon Friend that the gift with reservation rules will not be applied to an unconditional gift of an undivided share in land merely because the property is occupied by all the joint owners or tenants in common, including the donor.

What this means is, provided everyone pays their *full* share of the running costs (rates, repairs etc), giving away part share of the family home to your children so that they can live there has no adverse inheritance tax implications. It is *not* a gift with reservation.

'Leaseback' arrangements

Another more ambitious scheme involves dividing your ownership of the property into two separate legal interests and then giving away one of them. The overall effect is the same as if you gave away the property and then took back a long lease. However, the legal form of these arrangements are quite different since a leaseback arrangement of this nature would clearly be 'caught' by the 'gift with reservation' rules.

What actually happens is that a leasehold interest is created under which the owner is entitled to occupy the property, rent free, for, say, 20 years. The right to occupation of the property at the end of this period is called a separate legal asset and this is given away as a PET. Over a period of years the value of the lease interest gradually reduces and the rights to the property gradually increase in value by a corresponding amount. Once the seven years have elapsed, the only property which is subject to inheritance tax is the reducing value of the leasehold interest.

You might reasonably ask why arrangements of this nature are not also caught by the gift with reservation rules. In fact the Capital Taxes Office have given a limited, if grudging, clearance. The Controller was asked:

Could you please let us know whether the Inland Revenue intends to issue a statement of practice regarding the Revenue's view on various types of gift which they would treat as gifts with reservation under the new inheritance tax legislation. If not, could you please let us know whether or not the Revenue would regard the following type of gift as a gift with reservation . . .

D owns freehold property and grants a lease to himself and his wife for twenty years at a peppercorn. D then gifts the reversionary interest in the property to his son.

He replied:

If the true construction of the transactions here is that the gift to the son is of the reversionary interest only in the property then the gift would not constitute a gift with reservation.

These arrangements are sometimes called 'Munro' schemes because they rely on principles established in an estate duty case decided in 1934.

The legal aspects require very careful handling but this can, however, be managed. Once again it is the *personal* considerations which make these arrangements unsuitable for most people. What happens if you and your spouse (or just one of you) is still alive when the lease runs out? Could you then be turned out of your home? What is the position if you wish to move to a smaller property in five years time?

These worries would not arise if you could have a lease for life, ie a right to occupy the property for the rest of your life. Unfortunately, such an arrangement would not be covered by the *Munro* principle and the whole value of the property would attract inheritance tax on your death. In practice, what people do is to ascertain their life expectancy and them add, say, five years to cover themselves.

Another potential problem with these schemes is that your children etc may be subject to a swingeing capital gains tax charge when they sell the property after your death. There are ways of mitigating this but advance planning is essential.

As always, take advice from a specialist such as an accountant or solicitor.

14 Passing over the family business etc

Why trusts are especially useful

Trusts are especially appropriate where a person's wealth consists mainly of business property.

The most important thing for many proprietors is that they do not wish to relinquish control. This is one aspect where trusts are particularly useful. An obvious example is where a person who effectively owns 100% of the shares in his family company wishes to pass over 30% of the shares to each of his two sons. This will reduce him to being a minority shareholder and he is naturally anxious that his two sons may combine to outvote him on important business decisions. If he instead puts the shares into a trust for the benefit of his sons, and he and/or his professional advisers are the trustees, he can achieve the inheritance tax benefits without passing voting control into his sons' hands, although of course, as trustee, he must act in the interests of the beneficiaries and not just himself.

Very often, the proprietors of family companies take income out in the form of salaries rather than dividends. In such a case, a proprietor who puts 25% of his shares into trust for his children will notice very little change. He continues to draw his salary at the same level as before. If the company were to pay dividends some would now belong to the trust but it may be many years before dividends are actually paid.

Conversely, there can be situations where a trust is established precisely in order to pass over income. For example you

might establish a trust for the benefit of your grandchildren.
Dividends received by the trustees could then be used to
cover school fees etc and advantage be taken of the
grandchildren's personal allowances.

Trusts can have important non-tax benefits. Suppose you and
your son are in a farming partnership but you own the land.
You also have a daughter and you want to treat your children
equally. You therefore decide that you will put some of your
land into a discretionary trust so that your daughter may have
an income without you and your son losing security of
tenure. This may be a much more satisfactory solution than
if you leave half the land to your daughter who may then
sell it over your son's head.

Another possibility is that you want to start the seven-year
period running but you are not sure how your children will
work out. Perhaps your eldest son works in the company
and you want to see how he shapes up before passing over
control. The creation of a discretionary trust may be a very
good way of reconciling these conflicting objectives.

General strategy

We wouldn't want to give the impression that the *only* answer
to inheritance tax on business property is to set up a trust.
There is no *one* way of striking a balance between handing
over the business in a way that keeps inheritance tax down
to the minimum whilst protecting the proprietor's financial
security and ensuring that the business is run in accordance
with his wishes in the future. A lot depends upon factors like
the nature of the business, the need for capital and the
commercial risks involved, whether the next generation has
the necessary business acumen and experience, how far they
share their father's values and ways of dealing with things,
and so on.

There are also certain tax pitfalls, the financial equivalent of shooting yourself in the foot, to be avoided. Doing something which results in the effective loss of 50% business property relief can totally wipe out any benefit from an elaborate scheme, whether that scheme involves a trust or anything else. It is, therefore, very important to get the 'basics' right, and the rest of this chapter concerns the general strategy that you should adopt.

The main principles are as follows:

- Maximise the benefit of business property relief and the facility to pay tax by instalments. Make sure that any action that you take doesn't put these very valuable reliefs in jeopardy.
- Take steps to secure your personal financial independence before making any gifts.
- Consider how the effective use of insurance and pension arrangements can help you to cover the position in the short and medium term.
- All other things being equal, it may make sense for you to make gifts sooner rather than later, especially if the business is growing in value.
- The order and timing of gifts can have unexpected consequences, both good and bad, so take advice from your accountant or solicitor.
- As always, try to draw up your Will in the most tax efficient way that is compatible with what you want to happen to your money.
- Estate freezing schemes exist where most of the future growth in value of the business company, farm etc 'bypasses' your estate and accrues directly to the next generation. These are options that are sometimes worth considering.

We must go through these in turn:

Making the most of agricultural and business reliefs

There are some ways in which you could get less business relief than you would expect. For example, agricultural and business reliefs are due only on the net value after deducting any loans secured against the property in question.

EXAMPLE

Walter owns a farm worth £400,000. It is subject to a £250,000 mortgage so he gets agricultural relief on £150,000. If the loan had been secured on *other* assets he could have qualified for agricultural relief on the full £400,000. This can make a difference of £50,000 (the tax saving from the extra £125,000 of agricultural relief).

Exactly the same principle would apply if Walter had owned a business instead of a farm. As a rule of thumb any loans should be secured against non-business property.

Beware of buy/sell agreements

You might even find that your estate wouldn't be eligible for these reliefs at all. Many partnership agreements include a clause which is intended to protect the widow and family of a deceased partner. A typical clause in such an agreement states that on the death of a partner the firm's accountants shall ascertain the value of his interest according to certain rules, and the surviving partners shall then purchase that interest. Very often the partnership agreement requires each partner to take out an insurance policy for the benefit of his partners. They can then use the proceeds to buy out the widow.

Many private companies particularly those which are owned by two or three people who are not related to one another include similar provisions in their articles or the various shareholders/directors have entered into a shareholders agreement which has the same effect.

These type of agreements are a very sensible way of protecting your family who might otherwise be left with shares that do not produce any income. They are also a good idea for the surviving partners or directors since the last thing they probably want is to be working for someone else, as will be the case if the widow retains an interest in the business and effectively becomes a 'sleeping partner' or non-working shareholder. It must make sense for there to be a clear written agreement as to what should happen in such unfortunate circumstances.

There is, however, a problem in that the Revenue regard these agreements as tantamount to a contract for sale. As you may recall from Chapter 8, no business and agricultural relief is available where property is subject to such a contract.

Once again, this problem can be avoided. There is a legally enforceable arrangement which has exactly the same consequences as a buy/sell agreement but which does not entail the loss of business relief. The arrangement involves options. Your estate has an option to sell to the surviving partners/directors, they have an option to acquire that interest. In general, both options are worded so that they have to be exercised at market value.

Secure your own financial position first

Before you consider handing over your livelihood you should take steps to secure your personal financial independence. Only when you have this security will you be able to relinquish control. Achieving this is not as hard as it sounds. For example, the existence of a well funded pension scheme may mean that you can take a more relaxed view on handing over to the next generation. You certainly won't be pleased if they run the business badly but you will no longer have 'all your eggs in one basket' and your pension will mean that you won't go without in retirement because of mismanagement on their part.

The cost of doing this need not be unacceptably high, particularly if you start to take such action well before you approach retirement age. Also bear in mind that pension contributions are tax deductible and that, since the Share Valuation Division of the Revenue's Capital Taxes Office may well use post-tax profits as a yardstick, you will be helping to keep the value of your company's shares low for tax purposes.

Another way of approaching this problem is to enter into a long-term service contract with the company before you give away shares. Take care, however, to ensure that the Revenue cannot attack this as a reserved benefit as they will almost certainly do if the remuneration payable under the service contract is higher than the 'market rate' for your services.

The role of insurance

Insurance can play an important part in ensuring that adequate sums are placed in the right hands, and at the right time, in a way that is free from tax. The fact that an amount of up to four times your remuneration can be provided through the company pension scheme is sometimes overlooked. Also, if you do make lifetime gifts the recipients should seriously consider taking out seven-year insurance on your life to cover the tax payable by them if you die in this period.

Make gifts sooner rather than later

As with any assets that are likely to appreciate, the sooner you give such property away, the more will be achieved from an inheritance tax point of view. You have to balance against this the fact that you want to retain management control until the next generation are able and ready to run the business.

A lot can be achieved, even if you only give away part of your shareholding and retain overall control. The shares that you give away will continue to grow in value and, if you hadn't made the gift, the full amount would attract inheritance tax on your death.

EXAMPLE

Bernard owns 100 shares in Canterbury Ltd which are worth £2,000 each. He transfers 49 to his son, Michael, thereby, still retaining day-to-day control. Suppose the shares are worth £3,000 at the date of Bernard's death. If he hadn't made a gift, the full £300,000 would have formed part of his estate. Even if Bernard dies within the seven years of making the gift, £49,000 (ie 49 × £3,000 − £2,000) would escape inheritance tax completely.

Furthermore, making gifts can also open wider possibilities for tax savings through the way that shares etc are left in a Will. In the above example, Bernard could leave Michael further shares in his Will and this would be especially appropriate if such a transfer is covered by the nil rate band. By Bernard leaving, say, two more shares to Michael in his Will and the balance to Bernard's widow, he could transfer control with inheritance tax being assessed only on a further £6,000. So, overall, Michael will have been given a 51% shareholding as a result of the following chargeable transfers:

Lifetime gifts	98,000	
less 50% business relief	49,000	
		49,000
Two shares transferred on death	6,000	
less 50% business relief	3,000	
		3,000
		52,000

Alternatively, the 51 shares can be left to Bernard's wife who can make a PET in favour of Michael (but there must be no *requirement* that this must be done or it will fall foul of the anti-avoidance regulations – see Chapter 20).

Order and timing of gifts

The order in which gifts are made may have important consequences as is shown by the following example.

EXAMPLE

Suppose that Peter owns 51% of his family company and he has made no previous transfers. He decides to give 17% to each of his three sons but he decides to postpone the gift to the youngest son until he reaches 30.

When Peter makes the gifts to his two older sons the transfer of value will be as follows:

Value of 51% shareholding	250,000
less value of 17% shareholding retained	80,000
Gift	170,000
less business relief at 50%	85,000
	£85,000

However, when he eventually makes his gift to the other son the transfer will be assessed as:

Value of 17% shareholding	80,000
less 30% business relief	24,000
Total	£56,000

If Peter dies within seven years a total of £141,000 could therefore be assessed whereas if he could find a way to transfer 51% simultaneously the PET would be:

Value of 51% shareholding	250,000
less 50% business relief	125,000
	£125,000

Furthermore, because Peter's gift to the youngest son happens last the nil rate band would be allocated unfairly. Thus, if Peter died within the seven years the youngest son would be liable to pay £12,400 but his brothers would have no liability at all.

Peter could avoid this unexpected consequence by making the gift to his son at the same time as the other transfers and putting the 17% in trust until the son reaches 30.

There are also quirks or anomalies. Your accountant, solicitor or other financial adviser is best placed to identify these, but here is an example.

EXAMPLE

Suppose you own 45% of a family company and your family trust (in which you have an interest in possession) owns 40%. You wish to transfer 40% to your son. You should ask your accountant, 'does it make any difference if I give part of my shareholding or is it better to wind up the trust?'

The transfer of shares personally owned by you is taxed in one way; the transfer of shares passing as the result of the termination of a trust is taxed on an entirely different basis. It's an area where you should seek professional advice.

Gifts preceded by transfers to your spouse

EXAMPLE

Suppose you own 80% of the company and you wish to give your son and wife 40% each. An 80% shareholding is worth £280,000, a 40% holding is valued at £80,000. Does it matter if your wife or son receive their 40% first?

If you give your son his 40% first:

Value of 80% shareholding	£280,000
less value of 40% shareholding	80,000
	200,000
less 50% business relief	100,000
	100,000

If you give 40% to your wife first, you will together own 80% and under the related property rule (see Chapter 8) your combined value is £280,000. Your share of this is therefore £140,000. If you now give this to your son, the chargeable transfer is this value less 50% business property relief, ie a net transfer of only £70,000.

Once again, the gift to your wife is free of inheritance tax.

The Revenue might conceivably attack a transfer to your wife as an associated operation (see Chapter 19) but it is by no means certain that they would do so or, even if they did, that they would succeed. A reasonable delay between the two gifts could reduce the risk of such a Revenue attack.

We conclude this section by looking at another way in which a gift can have unexpected consequences. Suppose you give your wife the 40% and she immediately gives it to your son. Leaving aside the question of whether this now amounts to an associated operation, this could have disastrous consequences since she would not have owned her shares for two years and business relief would not be due if she failed to survive seven years. If she had inherited them from you she could take credit for your period of ownership but this does not apply where a person received ownership through a gift.

Drawing up your Will in an appropriate way

It is in the nature of some professions and businesses that a spouse cannot take over or employ a manager. For example, you may be a dentist, doctor or solicitor and you own your surgery, office premises etc. In such situations there can be a tax saving if the business property is *not* left to your spouse as it will form part of their estate on death and business property relief will not be available.

EXAMPLE

George dies leaving his entire estate worth £350,000 to Mary. It includes his doctor's surgery worth £150,000. Mary lets the premises to another doctor. Three years later she dies and inheritance tax of £96,000 is payable on her estate of £350,000.

If the surgery had not passed to Mary there would have been no inheritance tax payable as the position would have been:

Value of property	£150,000
50% business property relief	£75,000
	£75,000

This amount is covered by the nil rate band.

Because the surgery now forms part of Mary's estate and business relief is not available, extra tax of £60,000 is payable (£150,000 × 40%).

Depending upon circumstance it may be appropriate for the business property to pass to the children or other heirs. Alternatively, a discretionary Will trust under which the spouse can benefit may be the best way of utilising business relief.

Estate freezing schemes

This is an area where you need to consult your accountant or solicitor. For the businessman with his own company, the basic idea is to create a new class of share in the company. Very often those shares carry no rights to dividend or votes until a period of, say, ten years has elapsed. At that time they carry equal rights to the existing shares (or, as accountants put it, they 'rank pari passu').

Having created these new shares, you then give them away. The present value is relatively modest so the amount at risk if you die within seven years is not that much. The shares gradually acquire value so that after the deferred period they are worth as much as your original shares. This appreciation is not subject to inheritance tax as it accrues directly to the people to whom you have given the shares, and 'by-passes' your estate.

Some schemes work on a different basis and involve converting the existing shares into a special kind of preference share. The idea is that if the company makes profits of £100,000, and owns assets at present worth £500,000, the dividend and liquidation rights of the present shares shall be restricted to, say, a right to share in profits up to £120,000 and to take assets of £600,000 on a liquidation. Anything beyond this belongs to a new class of ordinary share. These new shares are likely to become very valuable eventually, but once again have only a limited value at the date of their creation.

There are similar arrangements whereby owners of farmland enter into partnership arrangements which transfer benefit to their children etc over a long period. The legal mechanics are quite different, and often involve entering into a lease over the land, but the object and the general principles are similar. Expert advice is essential as there is a minefield of anti-avoidance legislation. The professional costs involved in implementing such arrangements make them unsuitable unless you are talking about substantial amounts.

15 Planning in practice

The previous chapters have emphasised two aspects:

- the need to be cautious and to avoid the loss of financial independence
- the desirability of careful advance planning.

There is no single way of dealing with inheritance tax – the art is generally to use a combination of basically quite simple techniques in a way that best fits your personal circumstances and objectives. To show how much can be achieved we examine three fairly typical cases.

EXAMPLE 1:

Harold and Mary – surplus income in middle age

Harold and Mary are aged 63 and 58 respectively. They own the following property:

	Harold £	Mary £
Their home	100,000	(joint names)
Stocks and shares	70,000	30,000
Cash deposits	20,000	30,000
	190,000	60,000

Harold's Will leaves everything to Mary (and vice versa). On their death they want their property to be divided equally amongst their son and daughters.

Harold and Mary's gross income position is:

	Harold £	Mary £
Pension (index-linked)	15,000	–
Dividends	3,500	1,500
Interest	1,400	2,000
	19,900	3,500

In fact, they live off Harold's pension. From time to time Mary draws on her deposits but Harold's investment income is reinvested. In two years time they will become entitled to the State Retirement Pension.

At present inheritance tax would be payable only if they both die. The inheritance tax on their combined wealth of £250,000 would be £56,000. However, if they continue to reinvest surplus income they may well be worth, say, £300,000 by the time that Harold is 70. The inheritance tax could then amount to £76,000. The children could therefore expect to receive the equivalent of £224,000 in due course.

So what can be done?

Harold and Mary changed their Wills. Harold's Will now provides that £50,000 of his stocks and shares should go into a discretionary will trust under which Mary may benefit. The balance of his estate passes to her absolutely. Mary's Will now provides for her assets to pass directly to their children if she dies before Harold.

Harold and Mary decided to start giving away part of Harold's investment income. They allocated £2,500 for gifts (they can vary the allocation according to circumstances) and £1,000 per annum to go into a Joint Life Last Survivor insurance policy which should produce about £61,500 on the second death.

Harold and Mary's children will now, therefore, get

	£
From Lifetime Gifts (£2,500 per annum say)	25,000*
From Insurance Policy	61,500
Harold's Will Trust	50,000
Mary's Estate on her death	200,000
	336,500
less Inheritance Tax @ 40% on Mary's Estate	
less the Nil rate band	36,000
	300,500

* Obviously this depends on how long Harold and Mary live – and whether they continue to make annual gifts at this level.

EXAMPLE 2:

Val and John – passing on the family company

Val and John are aged 65 and 67. They have two main assets:

their home worth £150,000
a family company £500,000

Val and John hold 50% of the shares each. They wish to pass the company on to their son James who is employed by it.

The first thing to note is that due to business property relief the inheritance tax liability in total will not exceed £116,000. The amount which relates to the family company (72,500) can be paid by instalments over ten years. So the position is by no means desperate.

However, there are a number of steps that Val and John could take in order to make inroads into this.

For example, they could put their own finances on a sound long term footing by establishing a company pension scheme. They should ensure that the pension scheme will provide death in service cover up to age 75 as this will largely cover the position in the short term. Having done that, they might then each put 25% of the shares in the family company into trust for James. This would enable them to make a transfer without relinquishing day-to-day control as the voting rights etc would be held by the trusees rather than by James.

Suppose that John lives for seven years and that on his death his remaining shares pass to James and the matrimonial home passes to Val. This will probably mean that no inheritance tax is payable on his death.

When Val dies the position is likely to be as follows:

	£
Value of home	150,000
25% shareholding – say £125,000	
less 50% business property relief, £62,500	62,500
	212,500
Inheritance tax payable @ 40% on £212,500 less the nil rate band	41,000

EXAMPLE 3:

Christopher and Elizabeth – low yielding capital

Christopher and Elizabeth's situation is completely different – they are well off for capital but relatively short of income. They own the following property:

	Christopher	*Elizabeth*
Their home	£250,000	–
Antiques and pictures	100,000	–
Stocks and shares	–	35,000
Cash deposits	5,000	1,000
	£355,000	36,000

They have one married daughter who lives with them and to whom they are completely devoted. Christopher's Will leaves everything to Elizabeth (and vice versa).

Christopher's gross income from his pension is £5,000 per annum.

Christopher is now aged 70 and Elizabeth is 68. The scope for planning is limited by the nature of their assets and their income requirements. If they take no action the inheritance tax liability on Elizabeth's death (assuming Christopher had previously died) could be as much as £112,400. Equally worrying is that Christopher is very aware that his income is insufficient and is concerned that he may have to sell their home.

This is an ideal situation for Christopher to make a gift to his daughter of a half share of the family home. This should save inheritance tax of £44,000 in itself, and the fact that she will be responsible for paying half of the annual outgoings is very reassuring to Christopher.

Christopher might also transfer the antiques and pictures to Elizabeth, just in case she dies first. Elizabeth could draw her Will so that these assets would pass to the daughter.

Christopher might also draw his Will so that the daughter will inherit the other half share in the house on his death. This is obviously a big step to take and whether it was appropriate would depend very much on the relationship between Elizabeth and her daughter. Alternatively, the half-share could be left in trust for the daughter's benefit which could produce almost identical inheritance tax consequences.

16 The single person's perspective (and advice for those who have remarried)

Some readers will not have a spouse. They may be widows or widowers, people who have not married or who are divorced. There will also be some people who have remarried and who have children from a former marriage. All of these situations bring a different outlook. You still want to leave your money wisely but there are other considerations which do not concern the married couple with children.

Clearly a lot depends upon your particular situation, on how well off you are, whether you have close relatives or friends, whether you wish to hand on certain property which has been in the family for several generations. A person who has remarried will also often have to strike a balance between providing for his new wife (or husband) and passing capital over to his children by his previous marriage. We cannot hope to do more than sketch the main things which concern most people who find themselves in these circumstances.

Widows and widowers

If you have recently been widowed and have children (and grandchildren) we would advise you to take some time to weigh up your situation. Losing your partner after many years of marriage is a very traumatic experience and you must allow yourself time to get over the immediate shock. Your family will want to help you to get back on your feet and this is a time for letting other people do things for you.

After, say, a year has passed, take a detached view of your circumstances and ask yourself:

- How old are you?
- How long do you expect you will live?
- How long might you live?
- How well off are you for income?
- Might you remarry?
- How close are you to your children?
- Are they already well provided for?
- Will you want to move home?

Deeds of variation

We picked the period of one year advisedly. As you will recall, deeds of variation can be effected within two years of a person's death. You still have 12 months to enter into such a deed and give up part of the property that you have inherited from your late husband or wife.

Reread the section in Chapter 11 that deals with such deeds. If your partner left a large estate perhaps you can enter into a deed so that a good part of the nil rate band goes into a discretionary Will trust. Remember that you can be a trustee and a potential beneficiary of such a trust.

Your husband's pension scheme may provide a lump sum death benefit. Perhaps part of this could also go into a discretionary trust. Doing this will mean that you can receive income but the capital will not attract inheritance tax on your death.

Perhaps your spouse died and left more than the nil rate band. There could be a case for the Will to be varied so that your children etc give up *their* inheritance in favour of you. The idea would be that you could then make a gift or PET in their favour. This can be particularly attractive where a person died before 15 March 1988 and inheritance was payable at rates substantially in excess of those today.

EXAMPLE

Charles died on 1 March 1988 leaving Caroline his widow £200,000 and their children £250,000. If nothing changes, the inheritance tax on Charles' estate would be £62,000, computed as follows:

Total estate	450,000
less exempt as passing to spouse	200,000
	£250,000
First £90,000	Nil
£90–140,000 at 30%	15,000
£140–220,000 at 40%	32,000
£220–250,000 at 50%	15,000
Tax due	£62,000

This liability would be eliminated if a deed of variation were made so that Caroline took £360,000. The position would then be:

Charles' estate	450,000
Less exempt as passing to spouse	360,000
Passing to children	£90,000
Inheritance tax on £90,000	Nil

Caroline could then give the children £160,000 herself as a PET so that they finished with a combined £250,000, and no inheritance tax would be payable if she survived seven years. Even if she lived for only four years the maximum tax payable would be £10,000 because of taper relief. Tax of £20,000 could be payable on death before four years have passed but this can be covered by insurance (see below).

Professional advice should be taken to ensure that such transactions are not carried out in a way that allows the Inland Revenue to attack as 'associated operations', as mentioned previously.

Making lifetime gifts

Do be cautious. Your family shouldn't expect you to give up your financial independence. However, if you do feel able to give up part of your capital, get on with it to start the seven year period running.

Seven-year insurance

The above example is a classic situation where insurance is appropriate to cover the potential tax charge which will gradually reduce over the seven years. The cost of such insurance is not large in relation to the tax saving. For example, a woman of 70 could cover the potential liability of £20,000 for an annual premium of around £370.

Interest-free loans

It may well be a better idea to make interest-free loans (repayable upon demand) rather than give away a large part of your capital. This is less of an irrevocable step as the loans can be called back in and yet considerable benefit can be provided.

EXAMPLE

A widower aged 65 lends his children £30,000. They put this on deposit and use the income of £2,000 to pay life assurance premiums on a policy to cover their father's life. Cover of around £36,000 could be funded in this way and this would cover a large part of the inheritance tax payable on his death.

The unmarried person's perspective

The single person needs to be especially cautious. A person who passes over capital to his or her children and then finds that he has not enough income can look to the children for support. You must ask yourself the hard question, 'can I really afford to give this away and will they see me right if I have miscalculated?' On the other hand, a single person can sometimes take a more dispassionate view of things and draw on capital tied up in the home. Your house is an asset just like any other, and you haven't got to worry about passing it over to your spouse. For example, if you have to go into a nursing home your house could probably be sold to cover the fees once your other capital has been exhausted.

Some single people own family heirlooms. The best way to pass these on to nephews or nieces is by making a PET. Hopefully, you will visit them from time to time and share in the enjoyment of the property when you do so without it being a reserved benefit.

If you have a friend or relative who lives with you you may well wish to ensure that he or she can continue to use your home after your death. There are a number of possibilities here.

You might transfer a half interest in the property on the basis that your friend etc meets his or her share of the outgoings (see Chapter 13 on this). Alternatively, you might leave him or her the property in your Will and you can specify that the legacy is free of tax if you wish, in which case the inheritance tax will have to come out of the residue of your estate. Yet another possibility is to leave the property in trust so that your friend has the right to occupy it during his lifetime.

The remarried person's perspective

A person, who has remarried, often has to balance two conflicting objectives. He naturally wants to pass over capital to his children but equally he will want to provide for his new wife. In the past such people often drew up their Wills so that capital was held on trust. The widow was entitled to the income or enjoyment during her lifetime, and on her death the capital passed to the person's children.

This may still be the right approach for part of your capital. However, if you can afford to make alternative provision for your widow through life assurance this can provide a more satisfactory compromise.

EXAMPLE

Martin is aged 50 and married Sheila, his second wife, two years ago. She is aged 30. He has two children by his first marriage aged 22 and 26. Martin owns a house worth £250,000 and has a family company worth £200,000. He also has investments worth £100,000.

If Martin arranges for his family company to fund the maximum pension benefit and if he takes out insurance cover of £250,000 he will be in a position to leave Sheila only the house, with the shares in the family company and the investments passing to his children.

17 Foreign nationals

So far we have assumed that the person reading this book is domiciled in the UK. The basic rule for those who fall into this category (the vast majority of us) is that inheritance tax is charged on our worldwide estate, ie on property situated overseas as well as UK assets. In contrast to this, people who are domiciled abroad are generally subject to inheritance tax only in respect of UK property. The Channel Islands and Isle of Man count as abroad for these purposes. We need to go into some further detail on these rules.

Domicile and residence

These two concepts are completely different, and an individual can be resident (and *ordinarily* resident) in this country and yet be domiciled elsewhere. Equally, an expatriate may live and work overseas and yet still remain domiciled in the UK. A person may be resident in two different countries but he may be domiciled only in one country.

The concept of domicile is difficult to explain without going into legal technicalities. Basically, it can be summarised by saying that you are domiciled in the UK if you 'belong' here. The notion is that a person may be resident in a country for some temporary or limited purpose. For example, a person may reside in the UK whilst his children are being educated here or because his work requires him to be based in this country. Provided that he intends to return to his country of origin when those limited purposes are no longer relevant, then he is normally regarded as not having a domicile in the UK. Similarly, an English expatriate who is working abroad is generally regarded as having retained his UK domicile because he is only living abroad for a limited purpose (although that may, of course, last for 20 years or more) and he intends to eventually return to this country.

Domicile of origin

Domicile is not the same as nationality although having foreign nationality may be a very important factor in establishing that you have a foreign domicile. In law you normally acquire a domicile of origin which is the same as your father's domicile (unless your father dies while you are a minor or your mother is separated or unmarried in which case it is *her* domicile that counts). If your father changes his domicile before you become an adult (age 16 in this country) your domicile changes accordingly.

This domicile of origin will continue unless you acquire a new domicile of your choice. You do this by deciding to make your permanent home elsewhere with the intention of never returning to live in your country of origin except in so far as it is necessary for some temporary purpose.

It is extremely difficult to change your domicile. If the position is disputed by the Inland Revenue, the burden of proof lies with whoever is arguing that the domicile of origin has been abandoned.

Thus if you were born in England of English parents and your father is domiciled here (or was so at the time of his death) you are going to have an uphill task in persuading the Inland Revenue that you have acquired a foreign domicile. In contrast, if you were brought up by Italian parents and you regard Italy as your family home the Inland Revenue will find it very difficult to persuade the courts that your living and working here for 15 years means that you have become an Englishman.

Domicile a matter of intention

In part, domicile turns on something subjective – your long term intentions. The Inland Revenue always expects foreigners who have lived here for long periods to specify the circumstances that would lead to their leaving the UK and returning home. On the other hand, the facts about your way of life have to be consistent with your stated intentions and there may come a point where no reasonable person can believe that you have any firm intention of returning to that country. For example, an American living in Hampshire claimed that he intended to return to Connecticut when he was too old to run his farm here. Eventually he died here after being resident for over 50 years and the courts accepted that the intention to return to the USA was too vague and remote to count. However, that was an extreme case and there is nothing unusual about the Revenue accepting that foreigners who have lived here for 20 years are still domiciled abroad.

Married women

At one time a lady automatically acquired her husband's domicile when she married. Indeed, this is still the case if your marriage took place before 1 January 1974. It is now possible for a wife to have a different domicile from her husband, but obviously the standard of proof is high. Unless you can show firm evidence that you maintain your links with your home country and intend to return there (eg if your husband dies before you) the Revenue (and the courts) will tend to assume that you have adopted your husband's domicile.

Special rules for individuals who have lived in the UK for 17 years

The inheritance tax legislation contains special rules by which foreign individuals may be deemed to have a UK domicile for inheritance tax purposes. If you have been resident here for income tax purposes for 16 of the last 19 tax years you will normally be treated as acquiring a UK domicile if you are resident for the current tax year. This deemed domicile will then continue in force until such time as you are no longer resident for 17 out of the preceding 20 years. Having such a domicile will mean that your worldwide estate is subject to inheritance tax.

Take professional advice if you think you may technically be regarded as resident for some years simply because you had accommodation here available for your use. The criteria for residence may be slightly different for inheritance tax purposes so you may find you are not caught by the 17-year rule after all!

Can action be taken to avoid this?

There are indeed well-trodden ways of avoiding or mitigating these rules. One particularly common technique is for the person to set up a trust before the 17-year rule starts to 'bite'. We discuss this later in the chapter.

What assets are regarded as UK assets?

Assuming that you are of foreign domicile, and you are not yet caught by the 17-year rule, you may well want to know which of your assets will be subject to inheritance tax if you were to die now. The position is set out in Table 7.

Table 7: Assets chargeable to inheritance tax

	Not chargeable	*Chargeable*
Foreign property	√	
Channel Island property	√	
Isle of Man property	√	
UK property		√
Bank deposits outside the UK	√	
UK sterling bank deposits		√
UK foreign currency deposits	chargeable only if the owner is resident in the UK	
Shares in UK companies		√
Registered shares in foreign companies	√	
Bearer securities	depends where the bearer certificates are held	
Debts owed by a UK resident person		√ (normally)
Debts owed by foreign resident person	√	

Sometimes there is a double taxation treaty and professional advice needs to be obtained where large amounts may be at risk.

Do you have a foreign spouse?

As we have explained it is possible for husband and wife to have a different domicile. Suppose you are domiciled in the UK and your husband or wife is not (this could arise if you are caught by the 17-year rule but your spouse is not).

The position is that there is only limited exemption for property that passes to your spouse. At present the exempt amount is limited to £55,000.

EXAMPLE

If you die leaving property to your wife worth £250,000, and you had no other assets, the position would be:

Transfer on death	£250,000
less exemption	55,000
Chargeable transfer	195,000
less nil rate band	110,000
	85,000
Inheritance tax thereon	£34,000

Note that this restriction applies only if you are domiciled in the UK and your spouse is not. If you are both domiciled elsewhere, or if you are both caught by the 17-year rule, the exemption is not restricted to £55,000. Transfers from the non-domiciled spouse to the UK domiciled spouse are also completely exempt.

Extra planning possibilities

If you do have foreign domicile the UK may be a tax haven! Income tax and capital gains tax on foreign investments are often calculated on a very favourable basis and inheritance tax is generally a 'voluntary' tax – provided you do your tax planning before it is too late.

Foreign investment company

As we explained above, inheritance tax is not charged on foreign property if you have a foreign domicile (unless you are caught by the 17-year rule). In practice, it is easy for you to convert assets which would normally be UK property into foreign property since you can form a foreign company to hold UK investments, eg your UK flat or house. If your estate consists of foreign property and shares in a private company incorporated abroad, you have no UK property even though you may hold UK assets indirectly through the foreign company.

Such a company need not be incorporated in the country where you are domiciled. It can be formed in the Isle of Man, Channel Islands, Panama, Liberia, Liechtenstein, Switzerland – anywhere in fact apart from the UK. In practice, you will probably want to form the company in a country which does not itself impose death duties and which deals with income and capital gains in a reasonable way. Administrative convenience often leads people who are resident in the UK to use Isle of Man or Channel Island companies.

Getting round the 17-year rule

Simply holding no UK assets directly will not suffice once you are 'caught' by the 17-year rule and treated as domiciled in this country for inheritance tax purposes. Your worldwide estate will then be subject to inheritance tax.

In practice, however, it is possible to get around this by creating a trust before you are caught by the rule. If a person creates a trust with foreign property before he is deemed to have acquired a UK domicile, the property constitutes excluded property even if he is subsequently caught by the 17-year rule. The Inland Revenue have confirmed that this means that the transfer to the trust does not attract inheritance tax and the trust property is not regarded as part of a beneficiary's estate when he dies. Furthermore, the Revenue have confirmed that this still applies where the person is a beneficiary of the trust. The normal rules on gifts with reservation do not apply because the creation of the trust involves excluded property. You can, therefore, create a trust of the sort where you are entitled to all the income and the trustees have power to distribute capital to you.

Double tax agreements

Some countries have concluded double tax treaties with the UK which provide concessions for individuals who are domiciled in those countries. However, these tend to be countries which levy heavy death duties of their own.

Need for professional advice

There are traps for the uninitiated. Careful planning will reduce inheritance tax liabilities for foreign domiciled individuals but care must be taken not to run foul of other tax legislation. There have been cases recently, for example, where foreigners who are living in houses owned by their own foreign investment company have been assessed for income tax on a substantial annual benefit in kind. It is possible to avoid such pitfalls but you should take advice from an accountant or solicitor.

Getting away from it all

Perhaps after all this you feel you would like to cut the 'Gordian Knot' and emigrate ('surely doing this will eliminate my inheritance tax problems').

Necessary to establish foreign domicile

Unfortunately, selling up in this country and acquiring a home on the continent will not be sufficient. The worldwide estate of a person who is *domiciled* in the UK is subject to inheritance tax regardless of whether he is *resident* in this country. If you regard this country as your natural home, then you are liable to inheritance tax.

In theory, you might make out a case that you have abandoned

your original domicile in England and acquired a foreign
domicile. In practice, it will be an uphill task to persuade the
Revenue of this, especially if you continue to visit this
country regularly. Moreover, the Revenue may well withdraw
their agreement if you do later return to the UK and die
here, so it's no use thinking that you can establish a foreign
domicile, re-arrange your affairs and then come back to this
country.

The *Allied Dunbar Tax Guide* contains the following advice
on action you might take in order to establish a foreign
domicile:

- Develop a long period of residence in the new country.
- Purchase or lease a home.
- Marry a native of that country.
- Develop business interests there.
- Make arrangements to the buried there.
- Draw up your Will according to the law of the country.
- Exercise political rights in your new country of domicile.
- Arrange to be naturalised (not vital).
- Have your children educated in the new country.
- Resign from all clubs and associations in your former
  country of domicile and join clubs, etc in your new
  country.
- Any religious affiliations that you have with your old
  domicile should be terminated and new ones established
  in your new domicile.
- Arrange for your family to be with you in your new
  country.

Difficulties in acquiring a foreign domicile

In practice, the burden of proof is considerable. Even if you
are determined to do all that is necessary, do bear in mind
that the Revenue will not commit itself quickly. They will
want to be satisfied that you have become non-resident for
income tax purposes, since a person who is domiciled here
cannot acquire a foreign domicile unless he or she ceases to

be resident. Even when you have mounted this hurdle the Revenue will not give in, they will want to see whether the change in your way of life was merely temporary.

The difficulties are illustrated by the fact that a multi-millionaire with all the resources available couldn't achieve this change in status. The late Sir Charles Clore was the son of a Lithuanian emigrant who made shirts. He gradually built up a vast business empire but in later life he spent considerable time abroad and he made his home in Monte Carlo and sold his UK home. As far as establishing a new domicile was concerned, he had more going for him than most people. His family had only settled in the UK shortly before he grew up and when his business interests no longer required him to live here he moved abroad. However, he failed and the High Court held that he was still domiciled in the UK when he died.

The three-year rule

Another thing to bear in mind is that the inheritance tax legislation treats a person who has acquired a foreign domicile of choice as if he or she were still UK-domiciled for the three years following the change.

This has caught some people out.

EXAMPLE

Paul has spent most of his working life in the Middle East. He gets the Inland Revenue's agreement that he has acquired a Spanish domicile from 1 July 1987. On 30 June 1990 he sets up a discretionary trust with foreign property worth £300,000.

Normally a transfer of foreign property by a person who does not have a UK domicile is exempt. However, because of the three-year rule he is treated as if he were domiciled in the UK and the transfer therefore attracts inheritance tax.

18 Calculating the tax payable on death: a closer look at the rules

The purpose of this chapter is to go over the ground covered in Chapter 2 in the light of the information given so far. There are also one or two exemptions and reliefs that we haven't mentioned yet.

Let's start by looking at an exemption that could solve the problem at the stroke of a pen. It may be rare but there are probably one or two readers who might put in a claim.

Death on active service

Ever since the Second World War the death duty legislation has contained an exemption for a person who dies from wounds suffered whilst on active service. That must be right – if you are willing to give your life for your country you have every right to assume that the State will not penalise your family financially.

The exemption applies to the estates of those killed in the Falklands conflict and to estates of members of the RUC killed by terrorists in Northern Ireland.

The exemption may well apply more often than people think. Death does not have to be immediate, nor need the wound be the only cause of death. The High Court held in 1978 that the exemption was owed to the estate of the 4th Duke of Westminster because serious wounds that he had suffered in 1944 contributed to his death in 1967. Certainly you should consider claiming the exemption if a member of your family was wounded in the Falklands War or Northern Ireland and has died from a condition brought about by those wounds.

Other reliefs

There are some other reliefs we haven't yet mentioned. To put them into context we need to look more closely at the way in which inheritance tax is calculated.

Let's go back to the flow chart which appeared in Chapter 2 (and which is reprinted as Table 8 opposite), and have another go at calculating the liability which will arise on your death if you take no action.

We begin by looking at Box 1 – the net value of your 'free estate'.

The figures which you can now insert in Box 1 (see Table 9, page 152) may include three items where adjustments need to be made.

- valuation of quoted securities
- valuation of farmland and woodlands
- debts deducted in arriving at the net estate.

The first item, valuation of quoted securities, may require adjustment where the executors have had to realise part of the portfolio at a loss.

Sales of quoted securities at a loss

Relief is given where quoted securities or unit trusts are sold at a loss within 12 months of death. It is not possible to pick and choose – the relief is confined to the amount of any overall loss. Executors must in effect elect that the total proceeds of any sales should be substituted for the value at date of death.

Table 8

Husband	Wife

Box 1 Net value of your free estate £	Add	**Box 1** Net value of your free estate £	Add
Box 2 Value of settled property £	Add	**Box 2** Value of settled property £	Add
Box 3 Gifts which are clawed back £	Add	**Box 3** Gifts which are clawed back £	Add
Box 4 Chargeable transfers made in last 7 years £	Deduct	**Box 4** Chargeable transfers made in last 7 years £	Add
Box 5a Property passing to wife under your Will £	Add	**Box 5a** This property will form part of wife's estate when she dies £	Deduct
Box 5b This property will form part of husband's estate when he dies £	Deduct	**Box 5b** Property passing to husband under your Will £	Deduct
Box 6 Property left to charity £		**Box 6** Property left to charity £	
Box 7 – net total This is the figure on which inheritance tax is charged £		**Box 7 – net total** This is the figure on which inheritance tax is charged. £	

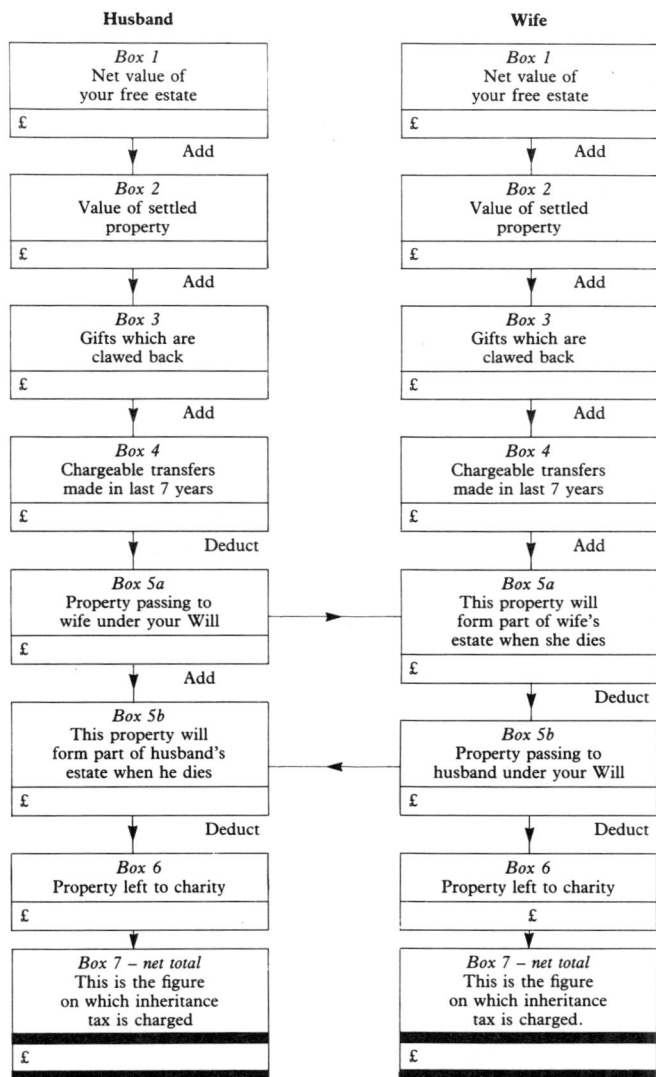

Basically one takes the figure in Box 7, deducts the nil rate band
(now £110,000) and the balance is charged at 40%. The tax actually
payable may be less if the TOTAL of boxes 3 and 4 exceeds £110,000.

Table 9: Box 1

> **Box 1**
>
> Net value of your
> 'free estate'
>
> £

This is made up as follows:

£

Cash at bank
    building society
Amounts owed to you
Quoted securities
Unit trusts
Insurance bonds
Insurance policies owned by you
Business property (see Chapter 8)
Shares in family companies (Chapter 8)
Farmland and woodlands (Chapter 8)
Your house or flat
Other investment property

less debts

Net value of your free estate

EXAMPLE

Angela died on 1 October 1987. Her estate included a portfolio worth £70,000. The executors had to sell some of the securities and realised an overall loss of £25,000. The estate can be reduced by this amount so that, in effect, only £45,000 is taken into account.

The *overall* loss of £25,000 may have been made up of a gain of £5,000 and losses of £30,000. Relief is, however, limited to the net figure.

Furthermore, the relief is restricted where the executors re-purchase quoted securities within two months of the last sale.

EXAMPLE

Angela's executors sold the securities on 14 November 1987. On 10 January 1988, they reinvested £10,000 in new securities.

The £25,000 loss cannot be claimed in full, it has to be reduced by 10,000/45,000 × £25,000, ie £5,556.

Sales of land at a loss

Relief is due where land and buildings are sold at a loss within three years of death, provided the loss is at least £1000 or 5% of probate value (whichever is less). The net proceeds are substituted for the value at the date of the death and the inheritance tax is re-computed. However, this relief applies only where the property is sold to an arms-length purchaser rather than to someone in the family.

Debts which may be disallowed

The Finance Act 1986 introduced a general rule that debts are not deductible where the deceased has made a capital transfer to the person who subsequently made a loan back to the deceased. This rule applies only to loans made after 18 March 1986 but there is no such time limit on the capital transfers. A debt may be disallowed because the deceased had made a capital transfer to the lender even though that capital transfer took place before 18 March 1986. It is also of no help that the loan was made on normal commercial terms and a market rate of interest was payable.

In Box 2 (see Table 10 overleaf) don't include anything for the value of any reversionary interests unless you acquired your interest by purchasing it. If the trustees sell quoted securities within 12 months or land within three years, the reliefs mentioned above may be claimed. Don't include anything for property held within discretionary trusts.

Table 10: Box 2

Add

Box 2 value of settled property.
£

This was covered in Chapter 5. You should write in:

£

Value of trust investments where
you have an interest in possession, ie:

Cash at bank
       building society
Amounts owing to the trustees
quoted securities
unit trusts
insurance bonds
Business property less business relief
Shares in family companies less business relief
Farmland etc
                      ————

less debts   ————

Net value of settled property   ————

Table 11: Box 3

Add

Box 3 Gifts which are clawed back
£

This was covered in Chapters 3 and 4. Complete the following:

£

Gifts without reservation since 18 March 1986.
Put down the value of the property at the date of the gift.
Deduct business or agricultural relief if the recipient of
the gift satisfies the requirements.
Deduct amounts covered by the
various exemptions set out in Chapter 3.
If you survive three years, taper relief
will be due (see Chapter 2). This
can't apply until 18 March 1989 at the
very earliest.

Gifts with reservation since 18 March 1986
Put down the value at the present time or at the time
the reservation ceased.
Deduct amounts covered by the £250 small gifts,
spouse and marriage exemptions.
Deduct business or agricultural relief if the recipient
satisfies the requirements.

In Box 3, don't put down anything for gifts made before 18 March 1986 – they go in Box 4.

The next four steps which are contained in Boxes 4–7 overleaf should be quite straightforward (see Table 12, page 156).

Legitim: special rules for Scotland

Something which will affect the bottom line is the calculation of spouse exemption. This can be particularly difficult where the deceased was Scottish as the 'legitim' rules need to be considered.

Scottish Law provides that a person must leave a set part of his estate to his children and their entitlement is called 'legitim'. If a person makes a Will which does not take account of this, the children can have it set aside. In practice children often decide to renounce their right to legitim, especially where a person's Will bequeaths all his property to his

Table 12: Boxes 4–7

Add

Box 4
Chargeable transfers made in the last seven years
£

Deduct

Box 5
Property passing to your spouse under your will or the provisions of a trust.
£

Deduct

Box 6
Property left to charity
£

Box 7
The amount that is charged.
£

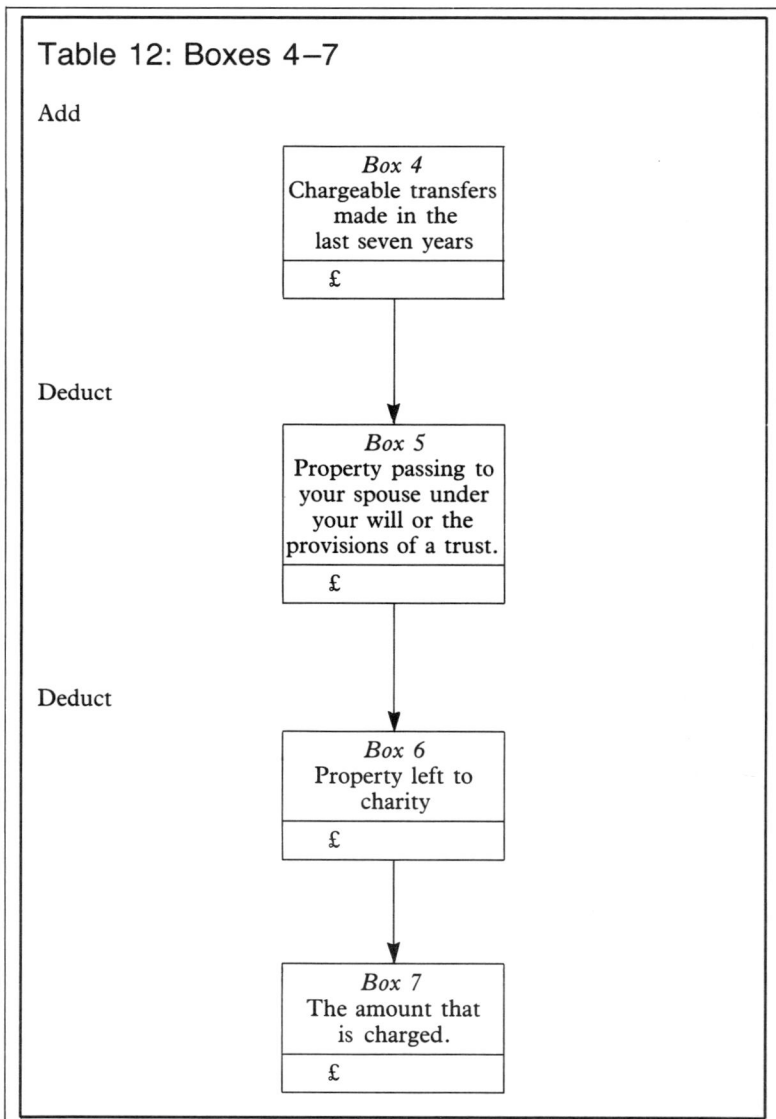

widow. The legislation provides that children who renounce their entitlement are not treated as making a chargeable transfer and the property is treated as passing to the widow in accordance with the Will.

Practical problems arise where children who are minors are involved since a child under the age of 18 does not have the legal capacity to renounce his entitlement. In such cases the executors have a difficult choice. They can either account for inheritance tax on the basis that the child takes his entitlement or on the assumption that the child will renounce his rights when he reaches 18. Let us look at the effect of each course of action.

Position where executors assume legitim rights are taken

Inheritance tax will have to be paid to the extent that the property which passes to the children exceeds the nil rate band. When each child attains 18 he may elect to renounce his rights so that the widow benefits. The spouse exemption will then mean that no tax should have been paid. The Revenue will then repay the inheritance tax paid and pay interest.

Position where executors assume that legitim will be renounced

No inheritance tax will be paid in the first instance. However, if it turns out that one of the children decides not to renounce his entitlement, inheritance tax on the death is re-computed and the tax payable attracts interest from the date that it should have been paid.

Quick succession relief

This is another relief not previously mentioned which may reduce the bottom line. Suppose you have recently inherited property from someone else. If you were to die and the full rate of inheritance tax applied, the implications would be quite outrageous. Perhaps the person who left you the property died before 15 March 1988 and, therefore, the former top rate of 60% applied. If 40% were to be payable on your death that would mean that the Inland Revenue had collected nearly 80% of the value of the property during a period of (say) two years. Even if both deaths attract only the current 40% tax charge, this still seems too heavy if the taxman is able to collect his slice twice over in such a relatively short period of time!

Quick succession relief is intended to alleviate this. The relief works by giving credit for a proportion of the tax charged on the first occasion against the tax payable on the second death. The proportion is set out in Table 9.

Table 9: Quick succession relief – credit for tax payable

	Proportion (%)
If both deaths occur within one year	100
within two years	80
within three years	60
within four years	40
within five years	20

EXAMPLE

A person inherited property worth £150,000 in June 1986. Inheritance tax was paid on that estate at an average rate of 45% so the grossed-up amount was £272,727 (£150,000 × 100/55) and the tax suffered was £122,727. The maximum amount on which quick succession relief can be claimed is 150,000/ 272,727 × £122,727 i.e. £67,500. This has to be reduced as two complete years have passed.

The recipient dies in August 1988. His total estate is £300,000 on which the tax is £76,000. However, the executors can claim a credit for £67,500 × 60%, ie £40,500.

The calculation of the relief is more complicated where the value of the property has gone down in the period between the two deaths.

The relief is not affected by the fact that the property has been sold or given away before the second death takes place.

There is also a measure of relief where tax is payable on a PET where the donor dies within the seven-year period and the recipient of the gift dies within five years. The computations can become quite complicated, especially where the recipient dies first, but the main principle is the same, ie that credit be given against the tax payable on the estate of the person who received the gift.

19 Reporting capital transfers and payment of tax

Lifetime transfers

An account on form C5 is usually required in respect of a lifetime transfer chargeable when made, eg a gift into settlement, where the sum of the gift and of any other like chargeable transfers made by the individual.

- in the same income tax year exceeds £10,000; or
- in the previous ten years exceeds £40,000.

Returns by executors

When a person dies his executors or personal representatives must complete a return to the Capital Taxes Office and pay the tax due on the assets disclosed in the return. Only when this has been done will probate be granted and until this happens the executors will not be able to take possession of the deceased person's property.

The reporting requirements are greatly simplified for small estates and an account is not usually required where:

- the total gross value of the estate for tax purposes does not exceed £40,000,
- the estate comprises only property which has passed under the deceased's will or intestacy, or by nomination, or beneficially by survivorship,

- not more than the higher of 10% of the total gross value or £2,000 consists of property situated outside the UK and
- the deceased died domiciled in the UK and had made no lifetime gifts chargeable to inheritance tax.

Even in such cases, however, the Capital Taxes Office may require an account if it is thought to be necessary. If an executor subsequently finds that he has made a mistake, and these limits were exceeded he is legally required to submit an account within six months of discovering this.

It often happens that the precise value of certain assets are difficult to ascertain and in such cases the executors may submit a provisional account which is subsequently revised. The fact that the account is provisional must be made clear to the Inland Revenue when the account is submitted.

Other returns

Other people may also be accountable, ie responsible for filing an account and paying inheritance tax:

- trustees in respect of settled property
- the recipients of lifetime gifts made by the deceased within seven years of his death
- any person who received a gift which was subject to a reserved benefit (see Chapter 4).

The time limit for making such returns expires 12 months after the end of the month in which the person died. The returns are required whether or not any tax actually becomes payable.

Errors and mistakes

When a person who is responsible for submitting an account finds that information that he has supplied is wrong in any particular, he is required to submit a new account within a period of six months.

Certificates of discharge

A person who is liable to submit an account and to pay tax may apply for a 'certificate of discharge'. This is given where the accountable person has submitted the necessary account and paid all the tax due. Once the Capital Taxes Office have issued this certificate, the Revenue are normally precluded from demanding further tax payments from that person.

A person who has received a potentially exempt transfer cannot apply for such a certificate until such time as the donor dies and the PET becomes chargeable.

Payment in kind

The Inland Revenue do have the power to accept certain types of property in satisfaction of inheritance tax liabilities. Such property includes pictures, prints, books, manuscripts, works of art, scientific objects or other items which are regarded as having national, scientific, historic or artistic interest. However, the Inland Revenue have to clear such arrangements with Heritage ministers and in practice only property which is regarded as of 'pre-eminent interest' is accepted.

If you do have a collection of first editions, antique snuff boxes etc which is acknowledged to be first rate you can find out more about these arrangements by obtaining a copy of '*Capital Taxation and The National Heritage*' which is available from the Inland Revenue Reference Room, Room 8, New Wing, Somerset House, London, WC2R 1LB (price £5.20).

When the tax has to be paid

The normal rule is that the tax is due and payable within six months of the death. Often however, the executors are not in a position to pay the tax by that time and interest then accrues from that date at a rate of (currently) 8%.

Inheritance tax on land and buildings can be paid by instalments over a period of up to ten years (or until the property is sold if earlier).

20 Anti-avoidance legislation

Every tax contains anti-avoidance legislation. This chapter outlines the ways in which taxpayers who rely on clever and ingenious schemes may be frustrated.

Associated operations

The inheritance tax legislation contains provisions which focus on associated operations. These are intended to 'catch' transfers of value achieved by a combination of two or more transactions and treat such transfers as if they had been achieved by a single chargeable transfer.

EXAMPLE

A controlling shareholder who owned 100% of the shares in a company might transfer 25% directly to his son and give 30% to his wife for her to pass on to the son. The effect is that the son ends up with a 55% shareholding. If it were not for the associated operations rule the use of the wife as a conduit might mean that the transfer of 30% would be measured by reference to the value of a 30% minority shareholding. The effect of the transactions being regarded as associated operations would be that the father would be deemed to have made a single chargeable transfer of 55% of the shares.

Definitions

Because this legislation is intended to prevent abuse the provisions were drafted in an extremely wide way. The courts do not give a taxpayer who strays into this field the benefit of any doubt. We must, therefore, look at the actual words of the legislation which define associated operations as any two or more operations (whether by the same person or by different persons and whether or not they are carried out simultaneously) which:

- affects the same property, or
- 'where one operation is effected with reference to another or with a view to enabling or facilitating the other to be effected'.

Furthermore, the legislation informs us that an operation includes an omission ie doing nothing could be just as dangerous as doing something.

On the other hand, the legislation sets out a specific exception. The granting of a lease for full consideration is not to be treated as an operation which is associated with any operation effected more than three years later.

How the Revenue interpret this in practice

So far there has been only one case that has come before the courts and the way that the legislation will be interpreted remains unclear even though it has been on the statute book for 14 years.

Some limited comfort may be drawn from a statement made in 1975 by the minister who was then responsible for capital transfer tax. He stated that a transfer of money from one spouse to another to enable the spouse to make a gift to a son or daughter would not normally be treated as an associated operation.

Unfortunately, the Inland Revenue do not wish to give any encouragement that goes beyond this. The Chairman of the Board of Inland Revenue was asked in 1978 whether the following transactions might be regarded as associated operations:

- A sells an asset to B but lets him leave the amount payable outstanding as a loan.
- In subsequent years A writes off part of the loan, possibly to make use of the annual £3,000 exemption.

The Inland Revenue view is that prima facie these are associated operations and the amount of the overall transfer might be assessed when the loan is repaid in full and by reference to the value of the property at that time.

Transfers made by close companies

Another aspect where the legislation contains anti-avoidance rules is that concerning close companies, ie where the shareholders refrain from action themselves and arrange for their company to make gifts or carry out transactions which transfer value to someone else. The legislation states that a chargeable transfer may arise where a 'close' company makes a transfer of value. Section 102 of the Inheritance Tax Act 1984 defines a close company as a company which is either director controlled or controlled by five or fewer 'participators' (normally shareholders). Most family companies fall within this classification.

The transfer of value made by a close company is 'apportioned' amongst the participators or shareholders, ie an amount attributed to each of them is treated as if it had been transferred by them personally.

EXAMPLE

The shareholders and directors of a company cause it to sell to Arthur an asset worth £500,000 for only £200,000. This is a deliberate attempt to give him a benefit. There are four shareholders – Peter, Paul and Philip each have 20% of the shares, Phyllis has 40%. Peter, Paul and Philip are treated as making a transfer of £60,000 each and Phyllis is deemed to have made a notional transfer of £120,000.

The apportioned amounts attract inheritance tax according to the circumstances of the different shareholders, but the inheritance tax is payable by the company. Normally, the amount apportioned to the participators will be added to their cumulative total of chargeable transfers but, where the proportion of the company's transfer apportioned to a person is 5% or less, the person's cumulative chargeable transfers are not adjusted.

Effect of alterations of capital

Where a close company's share capital is reorganised or there is an alteration in any rights attaching to shares or debentures of a close company and value is transferred, the alteration shall be treated as constituting a gift on the part of the shareholders.

21 Planning for your particular circumstances

One thing that ought to have come across in this book is that we all need to plan ahead. Leaving your money wisely doesn't mean taking action to avoid inheritance tax at all costs – far from it. What it does entail is:

1 Working out what is at risk (ie the inheritance tax payable if you do nothing).
2 Considering how you want to draw up your Will and whether there are ways of achieving these objectives which are more favourably treated for tax purposes.
3 Reviewing your insurance arrangements, calculating whether you have enough insurance and ensuring that the proceeds are going to be free from inheritance tax on your death.
4 Knowing if you have sufficient income to be able to make full use of the annual exemptions.
5 Deciding whether you can afford to make PETs. When considering gifts of shares in the family company, making sure you can retain a measure of control, for example, by creating trusts rather than making outright gifts.
6 Checking your conclusions by meeting with a specialist.
7 Reviewing your situation regularly. The Will that you draw up will need to be reviewed regularly in the future and, if necessary, amended to reflect changes in circumtances.

If possible, involve your spouse in these deliberations. After all, the way that she or he has drawn up their Will may have important implications. It may be better to talk through your situation with a professional in the first instance but if you are able to discuss your wishes with your children that will almost certainly help everyone to cope with the financial consequences of your death.

Choose with care your executors, and the trustees of any family trusts that you create during your lifetime. Ideally, they should be rather younger than you (but not too young), well versed in the ways of the world, businesslike and reliable in financial matters. If they are to have any discretionary powers, make sure that they understand your thinking. It may be helpful if you send them a non-binding letter of wishes every so often for them to consider when exercising their powers of discretion after your death.

There is no one way of leaving your money which is right in all circumstances. At the end of the day it must be *your* decision, but if you approach matters along these lines nobody will be able to deny that you have left your money in a careful and well thought-out way – in fact, wisely.

A glossary of terms

Accumulation and maintenance trust   This is a special type of trust where the class of potential beneficiaries is initially limited to people aged below 25. The trust deed must provide that at least one such beneficiary *will* become entitled to an interest in possession no later than his 25th birthday. See below regarding trusts generally.

Agricultural relief   This is a relief of either 50% or 30% which is deducted from the value of agricultural land in the UK, Channel Islands or Isle of Man. Certain conditions have to be satisfied, for example a minimum period of ownership.

Annual exemptions   There are two types of annual exemption. A person can give away up to £250 to any number of people in a tax year. This is sometimes called the 'small gifts exemption'. Quite separately, a person is allowed to make total chargeable transfers of £3,000 per annum which are treated as exempt.

Business property relief   This is a deduction of either 30% or 50% which is made from the value of business property when this is assessed for inheritance tax purposes.

Capital transfer tax   This was a tax on lifetime gifts and a form of death duty. It was in force from 1974 until 1986 when it was restructured and renamed 'inheritance tax'.

Capital Taxes Office   The department within the Inland Revenue that administers inheritance tax.

Chargeable transfer This is a gift, or a transfer of property on a person's death, which is not covered by an exemption.

Deed of variation Also called a 'deed of family arrangement'. This is a legal agreement entered into after a person has died under which the beneficiaries of his Will re-write its provisions.

Disclaimer A person may choose not to accept his entitlement under a Will or trust. A person who gives up his entitlement in this way is said to have 'disclaimed'. Provided certain conditions are satisfied the person who disclaims is treated for inheritance tax purposes as if he had never been entitled to benefit.

Discretionary trust This is a type of trust where the trustees can vary the way they use the trust monies and can choose how they pay out income to members of a class of potential beneficiaries. This is different to other types of trust where the trustees are bound to pay the income over to a particular beneficiary. See below re trusts generally.

Domicile This is a legal distinction which can be very important where a person transfers property situated outside the UK. A person generally has a foreign domicile if he does not regard the UK as his real home and he retains strong links with another country.

Estate The total of the property to which a person is entitled on his death, including certain trust property which is treated as belonging to the person.

Estate duty An earlier form of death duties. It was abolished in March 1974 and replaced with capital transfer tax.

Excluded property Transfers of excluded property are ignored for inheritance tax purposes. There are two main types of excluded property. A reversionary interest in a trust is normally excluded property. Foreign property owned by a person who is not domiciled in the UK is also excluded property.

Exempt transfers   Certain gifts or transfers on death are exempt.

Free estate   Property owned by a person, which he is legally free to dispose of as he wishes.

Gifts with reservation   A gift is not usually effective for inheritance tax purposes if the donor reserves a benefit. The property is treated as remaining in his estate for inheritance tax purposes.

Inter vivos transfer   An old fashioned term for a lifetime gift to another person. Property given away may be included in a person's estate if he dies within seven years.

Interest in possession   A person has an interest in possession where he is entitled to income as it arises from trust property. A right to occupy a trust property can also be an interest in possession.

Intestacy   A person dies intestate when he dies without having made a valid Will.

Joint ownership   Where two people own a property jointly. When one persons dies full ownership normally accrues to the survivor. See below regarding tenants in common.

Legitim   Rules which apply in Scotland governing the way a person's estate must be divided amongst his family.

Potentially exempt transfer (PET)   A potentially exempt transfer is one which will become exempt once the donor has lived for seven years from the date of the gift. If he does not survive seven years then the gift is subject to inheritance tax, but taper relief may reduce the impact.

Probate   When a person dies his executors have to file certain returns in order to establish their right to deal with the deceased's property. This is called 'obtaining grant of probate'.

Reversionary interest A person has a reversionary interest in a trust if someone else has an interest in possession and he will become entitled to the trust property when the other person's interest in possession comes to an end.

Settlement Another name for a trust.

Settled property When a person dies his estate consists of his free estate (see above) and property held in trust for his benefit, ie 'settled property' in which he had an interest in possession.

Taper relief Taper relief is a sliding scale which can reduce the tax payable where a person dies within seven years of having made a PET.

Tenancy in common This is a way whereby two or more people can own property. However, unlike joint ownership, each person can dispose of their interest in the property and ownership does not automatically pass to the survivor when one of the joint owners dies.

Transfer All gifts are transfers but certain transfers are not gifts. For example, when a person dies he is treated as making a transfer of all the property he owns. There are also deemed transfers such as where a person ceases to be entitled to an interest in possession. Unless these transfers are exempt they constitute *chargeable* transfers.

Trust Property is held in trust where trustees hold it for the benefit of clearly identified beneficiaries. The trustees must use the capital and income as directed by the trust deed and in accordance with trust law.

Index

Other titles in this series